D1535543

# Gymnastics
## FOR GIRLS

A gold medal guide
to great gymnastics!

**STEVE WHITLOCK**
*for the*
*U.S. Gymnastics Federation*

A *Sports Illustrated For Kids* Book

.
First Edition

Library of Congress Cataloging-in-Publication Data

   Make the team: gymnastics for girls / The U.S. Gymnastics
Federation. — 1st ed.
      p.   cm.
      "A Sports illustrated for kids book."
      Summary: Introduces the basics of girls' gymnastics, includ-
ing step-by-step instructions in the vault, floor exercise, uneven
parallel bars, and the balance beam; tips on training and conditioning; and information about meets and competition.
      ISBN 0-316-99794-3 (hc)
      ISBN 0-316-88793-5 (pb)
      1. Gymnastics for girls—Juvenile literature.   [1. Gymnastics
for girls.]   I. United States Gymnastics Federation.
GV464.M27   1991
796.44'082—dc20                                      91-14759

*Sports Illustrated For Kids* Books is an imprint of Little, Brown
and Company.

10 9 8 7 6 5 4 3 2 1

For further information regarding this title, write to Little, Brown
and Company, 34 Beacon Street, Boston, MA 02108

Published simultaneously in Canada by Little, Brown & Company
(Canada) Limited

Printed in the United States of America

Interior design by Goodman Leeds Design

Illustrations by Hayes Cohen

# CONTENTS

< 4 >

# CHAPTER 1

# IS GYMNASTICS THE SPORT FOR YOU?

More than 600 girls train at this gym in Houston.

< 6 >

**I** **T IS A DREARY, RAINY SUNDAY.** Your plans to go to the zoo with your friends have had to be postponed. Since you've finished all your homework, you turn on the TV and start flipping through the channels, trying to find something fun to watch. There's a golf tournament, a few old movies you've seen before, a news report, and some kind of documentary about spiders. But then you find a program that shows girls competing in a gymnastics meet. The announcer says the competition is called the American Cup and features gymnasts from the United States, the Soviet Union, China, Romania, Spain, and several other countries. This is more like it!

You watch as the girls perform unbelievable back flips, somersaults, and other tricks in events called the vault, uneven parallel bars, balance beam, and floor exercise. They make it look so easy and so much fun! Two of the American girls, Betty Okino and Kim Zmeskal [*zeh-MES-cull*], appear to be in a close race for first place in the all-around event, the one that combines all the events.

During a break in the competition, the program switches to a videotape of some of the girls from the U.S., and their coaches, practicing in their gymnastics club. The announcer explains that nearly 300 gymnasts train at the club. The youngest in the team program is 8 and the oldest is 17. A group of the younger girls is shown working with their coach on tumbling skills. They are really good! Some of the advanced gymnasts, like Kim and Betty, go to school in the morning and work on their gymnastics in the afternoon, but most of the gymnasts practice after school hours.

The TV program switches back to the last event, the floor exercise, in which Betty narrowly edges Kim for the all-around title. Since both of the girls' routines looked perfect, you wonder how the judges determined which was better.

As you continue thinking about them, you marvel about those tricky moves and what it would be like to join a team and experience the thrill of competition.

If you think that you would like to make the team in girls' gymnastics, you've come to the right place.

# What Is Gymnastics?

Gymnastics is, without a doubt, the most diversified of all sports. In fact, it is several sports rolled into one. Running, jumping, swinging, balancing, flipping, and twisting are just some of the activities and exercises that are involved. As a result, during a gymnastics class or practice session, all of the muscles of the body get a workout.

Gymnastics provides such complete all-around exercise that in many European countries a non-competitive form of gymnastics, called general gymnastics, is used as the basis for what we call physical education classes in the United States. After general gymnastics instruction, the European students go on to specialize in other sports, such as track, swimming, or even competitive gymnastics.

There are three competitive forms of gymnastics included in the Olympic Games. Women's artistic gymnastics includes four events: vaulting, uneven parallel bars, balance beam, and floor exercise. Men's artistic gymnastics is made up of six events: vaulting, horizontal bar, floor exercise, parallel bars, pommel horse, and still rings. The third Olympic gymnastics competition is a women's event called rhythmic sportive gymnastics, or just rhythmic gymnastics. Participants use various hand-held objects: a rope, a hoop, a ribbon, a ball, and a pair of clubs.

There are other forms of gymnastics competition not currently part of the Olympics. These include sport acrobatics (a combination of tumbling and balancing on one's hands), power tumbling (performed on a narrow tumbling strip), and the trampoline. In this book, our attention will be on women's artistic and rhythmic gymnastics.

# Why Gymnastics?

Gymnastics builds confidence and character—and it's fun! Whether you are the kind of person who enjoys exercise, fitness, or playing sports, or one who plans to dedicate herself to serious competition and rise to the highest level of her ability, gymnastics is for you.

Your self-confidence will increase as you learn body control. As you become involved, you will gain self-discipline. You will learn valuable lessons about exercise, eating correctly, and getting the proper amount of rest, all of which can lead to a life-long love of fitness and help you live longer and enjoy life to the fullest.

If you decide to pursue competitive gymnastics, there are various levels at which you can participate and gain recognition for your achievements. But most important, gymnastics is fun. More challenging than Nintendo? Certainly! More rewarding? Definitely! More fun? Absolutely!

# A Little History Lesson

According to ancient writings and artwork from the period, gymnastics began in ancient Greece and Egypt around 2600 B.C. Those are the first records of people participating in some form of tumbling and acrobatic-type movements.

What we call modern gymnastics began in Europe in the 19th century, particularly in Switzerland, Sweden, Denmark, Germany, and Czechoslovakia. In the 1800's, a German schoolteacher named Frederick Jahn built the first gymnastics equipment. Gymnastics events have been a part of the modern Olympic Games since they were established by Baron Pierre de Coubertin in Athens, Greece, in 1896.

But even though we call gymnastics in the 19th century modern, gymnastics today is much different from what it was back then. For one thing, the equipment (which we also call apparatus) used today is more suitable to the sport and safer than that used a hundred years ago. And in the past, men and women performed on the same apparatus. It wasn't until the 1952 Olympic Games that women's gymnastics was recognized as a different sport. There was a decision to eliminate the rings and substitute a new event for the parallel bars, events that had previously been performed by both men and women. This new event was called the uneven parallel bars. You will learn more about the uneven parallel bars and the other women's events as you read on.

Interest in gymnastics spread to the U.S. with the Europeans who migrated here. These Europeans organized sports schools that taught gymnastics. The German Turner clubs, the Czech Sokol clubs, the Polish

< 11 >

Falcon clubs, and the Danish Clubs are examples. From these clubs, gymnastics instruction spread to public school physical education classes and YMCA programs.

Gymnastics has become one of the most popular sports in the world. Today, more than 58,000 athletes are registered in competitive gymnastics programs in the U.S., with girls outnumbering boys seven to one. More than 5,000 competitions are conducted throughout the country each year. If we compare those figures with the ones in the mid-1960's, when barely 7,000 athletes competed once or twice a year, and when the only major international events for gymnasts were the Olympics and the Pan American Games, you can see how much the sport has grown.

A dramatic increase in interest in gymnastics has followed the crowning of each new Olympic superstar. In 1972, Olga Korbut of the Soviet Union thrilled the world with her daring skills and pixieish charm. Olga was followed by Nadia Comaneci [*NAH-dee-ya coe-man-EETCH*] of Romania in 1976; she demonstrated cool perfection and was awarded the first perfect score of 10. In 1984, Mary Lou Retton of the U.S. stole the show with her incredible athleticism and mile-wide smile. In 1988, the all-around title went to Elena Shushunova [*eh-LAY-na shoe-sha-NO-va*] of the Soviet Union, who showed that difficult maneuvers could be performed with dramatic elegance and grace. The world awaits the crowning of the new gymnastics queens at the Summer Olympic Games. The next

*Betty Okino is one of the top gymnasts in America.*

Summer Olympics will be held in Barcelona, Spain, in 1992, and in Atlanta, Georgia, in 1996.

# Competitive Gymnastics

Gymnastics is one of the few sports that is both an individual and a team competition. Unlike basketball or soccer, in which every player depends on a teammate in order to make a play, gymnastics allows a girl to compete on her own. At the same time, an individual's performance also counts toward her team's points.

There is nothing more rewarding than being part of a championship team. When Mary Lou Retton, the

< 13 >

1984 Olympic gold medal all-around champion, was interviewed immediately after the Games, she said that her only regret was "that we did not win the gold medal as a team."

# All Levels of Competition

The ultimate goal for every athlete is to participate in the Olympic Games. The Olympics are conducted every four years by the International Olympic Committee (IOC), an organization made up of representatives from most of the countries of the world. The United States Olympic Committee (USOC), in Colorado Springs, Colorado, represents the United States.

To keep track of the activities of all its participants world-wide, most sports have an international federation. Gymnastics around the world is coordinated by the Federation of International Gymnastics (FIG), in Moutier, Switzerland. The United States is represented in FIG by the United States Gymnastics Federation (USGF), headquartered in Indianapolis, Indiana. The USGF is the national governing body for gymnastics in the United States. It conducts activities and competitions in the sport and selects the coaches and members of the U.S. Olympic team.

The USGF was first organized in 1963. In addition to its administrative staff in Indianapolis, the USGF has a network of state and regional volunteers who work to make gymnastics a great sport in which to participate.

In the back of this book is the phone number of the USGF. The people in the main office can put you in touch with your state and regional chairmen. These individuals can tell you about the local and state USGF competitions (called meets) in which you can participate once you reach competitive levels. Meets are usually organized by local clubs or schools. There are also meets among YMCA's, public schools, and recreation programs, for which you do not have to be a USGF member to participate. All of these competitions are usually divided by age and ability groups, so that you compete against girls who are your own age and have similar experience to yours.

# How to Get Involved

Gymnastics has become so popular that there are now many ways to get involved. Dance schools, public schools, recreation centers, YMCA's, private gymnastics clubs, universities, and specialized groups, such as the Sokol and Turner groups we mentioned earlier, all offer gymnastics programs.

Talk to a school friend who you know is in a gymnastics class and ask her where she participates. Look in the Yellow Pages of your telephone book under "Gymnastics Instruction" and get the names of some clubs or programs near you. Or, call the USGF and ask for the name of the club nearest to where you live.

Once you have identified a few clubs or programs

that interest you, visit them and observe a class of girls your age. Then watch a team work out to see some of the girls who have progressed to a higher level. Are the girls having fun? Does this look like something you would like to do? Get as much information as possible on the program by asking the instructors questions like "How many students are in each group?" "Are the instructors safety certified?" (That means they've satisfactorily completed a course with the USGF.) "What special qualifications will be needed to make the team?" Talk to your parents. Discuss the costs and what the family budget can allow. Then make a decision as to which program seems the best for you.

The real trick is to get started. The decision of how far you want to go is up to you. In the beginning, body type, natural ability, coordination, flexibility, and strength will not play important roles in what you do, so have fun. Even if you decide to move on and try another sport, you will find that your gymnastics training will have provided you with skills and abilities helpful in your new interest. So, get started. The longer you wait, the more fun you are missing.

# Before You Begin

*Make the Team: Gymnastics* has been designed as a complete course in the sport of gymnastics for girls. Whether you're just getting started or are participating a bit and want to improve, you'll find what you need in the pages to follow.

But, please, remember this: Because gymnastics involves complicated movements and leaps through the air, frequently off high pieces of equipment, it is not a sport to be learned without a qualified teacher.

This book is intended as an introduction to the sport, to be used along with the lessons you learn in a gymnastics class. **Do not try to perform any of the movements described here, nor any gymnastics movements, with only this book and the mattress in your bedroom.**

Okay, let's do it!

< 17 >

# CHAPTER 2

# GETTING STARTED

**S**O, YOU'VE DECIDED THAT gymnastics is for you. Great. Now, let's get started on learning about different programs, what kinds of equipment are needed, and the rules of safety.

## How to Choose a Program

There are four factors you and your parents should consider when deciding on which gymnastics class you should enroll in. These are the physical setup of the gym, the degree gymnasts in the class seem to enjoy the program, the experience and credentials of the coaches and training staff, and the use of what are called progressions in teaching gymnastics skills.

The gymnasium should have plenty of space so that the gymnastics equipment can be arranged safely and efficiently. You wouldn't want to come vaulting off the horse right into the middle of someone else's floor

< 18 >

Good coaching can be the key to a good program.

< 19 >

exercise routine, would you? The environment should be well lighted, clean, and quiet. Do you like the way the gym looks?

If possible, observe a class before you enroll in it. Then you will be able to get a good feel for the way the class is conducted, the teaching style of the coaches, and the look of the students—they should appear to be enjoying the class!

The coaches should be knowledgeable and experienced. In addition, they should encourage their students' goals as gymnasts, as well as help them develop self-confidence and physical fitness. Do the instructors insist that their students master the beginning skills before they move on to the more difficult ones? Have they been trained in proper safety techniques?

Finally, the coaches' method of teaching should be based on the "progression system." This is a step-by-step method of teaching gymnastics skills one small movement at a time. The proper use of progressions by your coach is important in making certain that you learn gymnastics skills correctly and in as safe a way as possible. We'll talk more about progressions later in the chapter.

# Your Personal Equipment

No reason to buy a sixty-dollar baseball glove or a hundred-dollar pair of basketball shoes here. All you need to wear in gymnastics is a leotard and some kind of foot covering. Cotton footies, cotton socks, or special

< 20 >

gymnastics slippers made from leather or nylon are all fine. Some girls like to wear tights when they practice gymnastics; be careful if you do because these might be slippery on the beam or bars.

A warm-up, or athletic, suit would be a useful addition to your gymnastics wardrobe. It will keep you warm while you are stretching at the beginning of class or during practice. You can take it off when you are ready for your first event and put it back on while you are waiting for your next event.

Gymnastics clothing should fit snugly, without interfering in any way with your movement. It should not have loose ends that could become tangled on you or the equipment.

Jewelry should not be worn during gymnastics. That includes rings, necklaces, bracelets, watches, and earrings. Jewelry can catch on clothing or on an apparatus, which can result in injuries. Unless your club provides a safe to lock up your belongings, it is a good idea to leave your jewelry and other valuable possessions at home on gym days.

Likewise, your hair should be worn in a style that will not block your vision or become caught in the apparatus. Hair clips and barrettes, sharp and made of hard material, should be avoided. They hurt when you roll onto them, and they can loosen and land in your eyes. Competitive gymnasts like to experiment with hairstyles that look good and keep their shape while the gymnasts perform their events.

Once you start practicing on the uneven bars, you

< 21 >

will probably want to purchase handgrips. Handgrips prevent the palms of your hands from getting blisters and "rips" (open blisters). They are made from a variety of materials, but leather is the most common. Ask your coach to help you select the right size and show you how to use them correctly.

You will also use chalk at the bars to protect your hands. Your coach will show you the amount of chalk to rub onto your hands that provides the right tension for gripping the bars.

# A Tour of the Gym

The apparatus for women's gymnastics are the vaulting horse and board, the uneven parallel bars, the balance beam, and the spring floor for floor exercise. These will be described in detail in the following chapters. However, you will use many other kinds of special equipment and apparatus when you are learning gymnastics.

## The Mats

Mats are the most basic equipment in gymnastics; they are used in every event. You will be surprised at the number of sizes and shapes they come in, but they all perform the important work of providing safety.

There are two types of mats. Resilient mats, which are firm and bouncy, are used in tumbling and in floor exercise to help you gain height. Shock absorbent mats, which are thicker and softer, are used under apparatus and in landing areas to give greater protection for dismounts or a fall.

Part of your gymnastics training will include using mats properly. Before you perform a gymnastics skill, make sure that you and your coach have selected the right kind of mat and that it is placed correctly. When you are learning new or difficult skills, it may be a good idea to use additional mats. In later chapters of this book, you will see how additional mats can be helpful in learning tumbling and balance beam skills.

It is important to remember that even the biggest and softest mat cannot completely eliminate every possibility of injury. If you land incorrectly, such as on your head or neck or back, a serious injury can result on any type of mat. That's why it's important to learn each skill carefully.

Over the past few years, mat manufacturers have been producing mats in various sizes and shapes, like wedges, trapezoids, blocks, etc. These are called skill-builder developmental mats. The use of these special mats will help you learn basic skills more easily, quickly, and safely. For example, you might use an incline mat when learning a backward roll or a trapezoid mat for vaulting before you tackle the horse.

## Pits

Pits are another kind of gymnastics teaching aid. They can be built either above the ground or placed "in-ground." There are two kinds: solid-foam pits and loose-foam pits.

*Kim Zmeskal was the U.S. champion in '90 and '91.*

Solid-foam pits are like giant mats. They might be up to three feet deep and 20 feet long and are very soft. Loose-foam pits are like swimming pools filled with thousands of foam pieces. It is important that the foam is fluffed up frequently because the foam pieces can compress. After a while, a soft pit becomes a hard pit.

Pits were designed to provide a safer area for gymnasts to land on when learning new skills. But be careful! You can still get injured in a pit if you don't follow the safety rules your coaches teach you.

Even though pits allow for safe landings, some positions can result in serious injury. Never land head first, on your face or on your chest, or with your back in an arched position. Do not wear jewelry, clothing accessories, or hair clips when using a pit. If any of these items fall into the pit, they could injure the next person. And of course, check to see if anyone else is in the pit before you drop in.

# Playing It Safe

Gymnastics is fun and one of the best overall physical fitness activities that there is—provided that you and your coach use common sense and pay attention to the rules of safety.

After all, the sport involves flipping and twisting, sometimes from an apparatus that is very high. Therefore, by its very nature, gymnastics carries a risk of physical injury. No matter how careful you and your coach are, no matter how many spotters are used, no matter at what height the equipment is set or what landing surface exists, the risk cannot be eliminated. Reduced, yes, but never eliminated.

The risk of injury in gymnastics includes minor injuries such as bruises, and serious injuries, such as broken bones, dislocations, and muscle pulls. Unfortunately, as in practically every sport, the risk also includes very serious injuries, such as permanent paralysis or even death from landings or falls onto the back, neck, or head.

So you can see that it is important for you to learn

gymnastics from a good coach in a well-equipped gym and to listen carefully to your coach and follow the safety rules that your gym has set.

Just like the circus trapeze artist who always checks her own rigging before a performance or the parachute jumper who makes sure that she packs her own chute before a jump, there are things that you can do to make sure that your participation in gymnastics is safe:

• Never participate unless you have a proper supervisor. Every gymnastics class, practice, or workout should be supervised by a trained teacher or coach.

• Dress appropriately. Use chalk, handgrips, tape, and protective body equipment where needed. When in doubt, consult your instructor.

• Double-check your equipment. Before every session, be sure the apparatus is in proper working condition and is adjusted for your size. Also, be sure to have enough mats in the proper places. When in doubt, consult your instructor.

• Communicate clearly with your coach. Make sure that you both know exactly what, when, where, how, and why you are to perform a particular skill and how you will be spotted. If you have questions, ask!

• Be sure that you are feeling physically, as well as mentally, at your best and ready to perform. Total fitness is very important for safe gymnastics.

• Master the basic skills first. Don't try to skip ahead and move too fast! Follow the steps your teacher lays out for you to learn skills. Be sure to know the skill. This includes having a clear idea of what the skill is and knowing how to begin, execute, and complete the entire movement.

• Always follow through. Once you commit to performing a skill, follow through to its completion.

• Finally, know your limitations. You should develop a healthy awareness and respect for what you can do and what you cannot do in learning and performing gymnastics. Don't be impatient. There is plenty to learn and plenty of time in which to learn it.

# Learning by Progression

As we said earlier, the best way to learn gymnastics is through progressions. A progression is a step-by-step method of learning skills, beginning with the easy ones and gradually mastering the more difficult ones.

Let's use the teaching of tumbling as an example of how progressions work. Tumbling is considered the basis of all gymnastics. Although it is not one of the four Olympic competitive events, tumbling is important because the skills you learn will help you perform the other events. For example, the basic forward roll can also be performed on the balance beam and in the floor exercise, and is important even when learning the vault and the uneven bars!

Now, if you wanted to learn a forward somersault, you wouldn't just start out trying to do the somersault! Instead, you would learn a whole series of skills, one by one, moving along to the next one only after you'd mastered the first. For example:

*1. A forward roll down an incline or a wedge mat*

*2. A forward roll on a level mat*

*3. A diving forward roll onto a skill cushion*

*4. A three-quarter somersault onto a high stack of skill cushions*

*5. A forward somersault onto a landing mat with a spot by your coach*

*6. A running forward somersault without a spot*

< 28 >

It is important that you be patient when learning gymnastics through progressions. Don't move on to the next skill in the progression until you and your coach have determined that you are ready. This method will allow you to learn a large number of skills while having fun and developing confidence.

If you find a skill to be particularly difficult to learn, perhaps you are trying to take too big of a step, or too many, in your progression. Ask your coach for assistance. She or he can almost always give you smaller steps that will help you reach your goal.

# Talking the Talk

You will find that learning gymnastics (or any other sport) requires that you also learn the language of the sport. The language of gymnastics is quite complicated! For example, you will learn that a forward roll is done on the ground, but a forward somersault (or "salto") is done in the air. Your friends might think that you have learned a front flip, but you will know that this is really a salto!

All of the gymnastics terms used in *Make the Team: Gymnastics* are included in the glossary at the end of the book. Soon you will find that you "speak gymnastics" as well as an expert!

# CHAPTER 3

# VAULTING

**I**T WAS A VAULT THAT MADE Mary Lou Retton famous. At the 1984 Olympics in Los Angeles, Mary Lou and Ecaterina Szabo [*cat-er-EEN-a ZAH-bo*] from Romania were locked in a duel for the gold medal in the all-around event. The two gymnasts had stayed close to each other through the compulsory and optional events; it all came down to the vaulting event. If Mary Lou could score a perfect 10 on her vault, she would be the new Olympic all-around champion. Mary Lou was known as one of the best vaulters in the world but she often had trouble "sticking" her landing (holding still in place).

Mary Lou got the green light from the judges to start. She started her run, hit the board, and pushed from the horse to perform her chosen move: a full twisting Tsukahara [*zook-a-HAHR-a*]. She was perfect in flight and perfect in landing. The score was 10. Mary Lou was the new Olympic all-around champion!

< 30 >

*Vaulting is the gymnastics event most like flying.*

Mary Lou said that she knew she had the vault from the moment she started her run. She had made all of the preparations, and now it was time for everything to come together. And it did!

# A Horse Is a Horse, of Course

The apparatus used in vaulting is called the horse. It gets its name from an early form of gymnastics when soldiers actually vaulted onto and over real horses! Vaulting is one of the oldest gymnastics events that is still performed in the Olympic Games by both men and women.

As we mentioned in chapter one, in the early days of competitive gymnastics, men and women used the same equipment. But as the sport progressed, changes in the events were made to accommodate the physical differences between the sexes and to emphasize the artistic qualities of women's gymnastics and the strength qualities of men's. In men's gymnastics, in what is called Long Horse Vaulting, the horse is positioned for the gymnast to vault over it lengthwise. In women's gymnastics, the horse is positioned for the gymnast to vault over it sideways.

The body of the "female horse" is 14 inches (35 centimeters in the metric system) wide and five feet (160 cm) long. It is made of wood, or a combination of wood and steel, wrapped with padding and covered with leather or a synthetic material. The covering has a non-skid surface.

In international gymnastics competition and in the U.S. senior age division, the height of the horse is set at 47.25 inches (120 cm) above the floor. However, gymnasts competing in Junior Olympic competitions are allowed to lower the horse depending upon their age. That is, girls in the junior division (ages 12-14) are permitted to vault with the horse 45.25 inches high, and those in the children's division (ages 9-11) can lower the horse to 43.25 inches.

The horse is positioned at the end of a runway that measures three feet wide and between 78 and 82 feet long. The landing area is set up on the opposite side of the horse with mats that can be up to 10 inches thick.

The vaulting springboard is also called a Reuther [*ROO-ther*] board, after the man who designed it, and uses a spring device to help the gymnast jump to the horse. The board is four feet long and three feet wide. Its slanted design allows the gymnast to transfer the speed built up during the run into the height she'll need to make the jump from the board to the horse.

The gymnast may position the board at the distance from the horse best for her. Most gymnasts choose to place it approximately four feet up the runway from the horse. Gymnasts have also found that the best spot to jump from the board is about one foot from its far, or high, end because that point generally gives them the most spring.

# Ready for Serious Air Time?

Of all the events in gymnastics, vaulting is the one most like flying. The best vaulters explode off the horse, getting their feet up over their heads with tremendous quickness as they jump from the springboard to make contact with the horse. Instantly, they push off the horse and soar through the air, traveling at the great height and distance that allow them to perform a number of saltos and twists. Someday soon, you'll be able to fly, too.

Because you only have to perform one or two kinds of vaults at a gymnastics competition, you won't need to learn as many different tricks in vaulting as you will in the other events. But that doesn't mean vaulting is easy. The characteristics of a good vaulter (strength, speed, quickness, explosiveness, and even courage) all take time and preparation to develop.

Courage, confidence, and consistency—the three C's—are essential ingredients in becoming a good vaulter. Imagine the first time you are standing at the end of the runway looking down the distance and seeing a horse that is almost your own height. As you learn gymnastics using step-by-step progressions, eventually the horse won't appear to be so big an obstacle. By the time your coach expects you to perform an actual vault, you will be ready and confident.

# Performing the Vault

So, let's get to it. The vault can be divided into five different parts.

## Approach, or Run

After receiving the signal from a judge to start, the gymnast begins by running down the runway toward the vaulting board and horse, picking up speed as she goes. Because of the limited length of the runway, and her own stride length, she has only about 13-15 running steps to reach full speed by the time she reaches the board.

Speed is important. Just as in baseball, where the pitcher must have enough speed and strength in his arm motion to reach the catcher's mitt with his throw, the gymnast is basically throwing her own body. The faster she can run and the more powerfully she can jump from the board, the greater the height and dis-

< 34 >

tance she will reach in her vault. In general, the gymnast who flies higher and lands farther from the horse will get a higher score from the judges.

To learn how to run fast and efficiently, you will practice many of the drills and exercises sprinters use to prepare for track events. These include jogging, sprinting, coordination drills, and plyometrics, which is a new training method that can help increase the height of a jump. You will learn how to make your arms swing more powerfully and how to lift your knees and develop a consistent and powerful leg stride when you run; in the process, you will develop strength and endurance. Although the drills are hard work, they are fun, too! For example, you will have running contests with your teammates.

Your coach will probably use a stopwatch to time your sprints over a measured distance, like 20 meters, which is about the length of the runway. At first your times will be fairly slow. But as you learn proper running techniques, you will see your times drop dramatically. Experienced vaulters usually run the 20-meter distance in less than four seconds. It will probably take months, or even years, to get that fast. However, you will begin to notice improvement soon.

## Hurdle and Takeoff from the Vaulting Board

As the gymnast completes her run, she takes one final step, called the hurdle. In the hurdle, the gymnast leaps into the air to land with both feet on the vaulting board. This is a critical part of the vault.

The gymnast must judge her running distance just right so she lands on the board about one foot from the high end (the end of the board nearest the horse). As we mentioned earlier, this point on the board provides the most spring. Therefore, it gives the gymnast the biggest boost in her jump from the board to the horse, which is called the preflight. You will practice the hurdle-step until you have it just right.

The jump from the board that begins the preflight is called the takeoff. This should be a quick and explosive jump. You will learn how to coordinate your jump with the way you swing your arms out and reach for the horse. That will help you get the most power out of the speed you built up during your run.

## Preflight

As we said, the jump from the board until the gymnast first touches the horse itself is called the preflight. This is the first part of the vault that the judge evaluates (she does not evaluate your run).

During the preflight, you must get your body into the correct position to perform the vault you selected. (Later in this chapter, we will discuss some of the vaults you will be performing.) This position is important because it helps determine the height and distance of your flight off the horse, when you really do your stuff. That is called the afterflight. In general, a low preflight position will result in a higher afterflight and a high preflight will result in a lower afterflight. A higher afterflight is better because it will give you more time and distance in which to perform your acrobatics. A short, low afterflight will result in a deduction in your score from the judges.

## Repulsion

This is the part, also called the block, when your hands actually hit the horse. It comes between the preflight and the afterflight when you are trying to take your speed from the run and turn it into height in the vault.

The height you get is determined by the angle at which you arrive on the horse and how hard you push off the horse, using your hands, arms, and shoulder muscles. You will practice many handstand drills and exercises to make your shoulders strong. A strong and quick push off the horse from your hands will give you good height to perform the next part of the vault.

## Afterflight

This part of the vault includes everything the gymnast does from the time she leaves the horse until she lands on the mat. The afterflight is what the judges concentrate on; it is the most important part of the vault.

Just as in diving, where the approach on the board or platform might be similar for very different dives once the diver takes flight, gymnasts can execute different vaults from similar preflight positions. For example, a beginning gymnast might perform a basic handspring vault (more on this later), while an advanced gymnast might perform a handspring vault in pike position with a half twist. The difference is in the afterflight.

After you have nailed down the first parts of the vault, you will spend time working on special drills to improve your afterflight. These include air-awareness drills, which teach you how to keep your bearings while you're flipping in the air or flying through space; work on the trampoline and mini-trampoline; and basic tumbling skills.

More advanced vaults will be taught with advanced learning progressions and special training aids, like the gymnastics pit we talked about in chapter two.

## Landing

The goal is a perfect "stick"—a two-point landing without additional steps. If you take a step or more, or fall, on the landing, the judges deduct points from your score. (We'll talk more about scoring later.)

Learning how to land properly is a critical skill for the gymnast. Some landings are planned; others are not. Gymnastics is a sport with a great many kinds of movements performed at fast speeds. The movements generate a lot of force. Therefore, it is essential that a good landing technique be practiced until it is automatic. The special landing skills and drills your coaches introduce during your vaulting training will help you learn to land properly—and safely—in the other events, too.

In gymnastics, we often refer to landing in a demi-plié position. This is a modified dance term that refers to a landing on the full foot with the knees bent to absorb the shock of the landing. It is  important that you never land with your knees locked, which can injure them. Land first on the balls of your feet and then on your heels, in an almost flat-footed landing, and bend at the ankles, knees, and hips. Use your outstretched arms to control your balance.

It is fun to practice sticking, and you can have contests with others in your group. A popular gymnastics game is STICK-IT. This is similar to a game called HORSE played by basketball players when practicing shooting. One gymnast might do a vault in a tuck position. If she sticks the landing, the other gymnasts in her group have to do the same jump. If they also stick the landing, they get to move on without penalty. If they fail to stick, they get the letter *S*, then *T*, the *I*, and so on. Once one of you has all the letters in the STICK-IT, she is out. The last person left wins.

# A Vault Full of Vaults

Vaults are divided into four families:

1. Handsprings, including cartwheels and Yamishitas [*yahm-eh-SHEET-ahs*], which are handsprings that feature 90-degree pikes in the afterflight;

2. Forward saltos, with and without twists;

3. Backward saltos, with and without twists;

4. Vaults performed from a roundoff onto the board, which means the gymnast performs a cartwheel to

take off from a backward position (the other families used a forward takeoff position).

There are also vaults that don't fall into these families; these are basic, beginning vaults not used in international competition. Three of these, the squat, the stoop, and the straddle, are covered below.

The level of difficulty assigned to each vault is the highest score that a gymnast can receive for performing that vault. Generally speaking, the more saltos and twists involved in performing a vault, the higher its difficulty rating.

To give you an idea of how the valuing system works, we've compiled the table below, which lists some of the commonly performed vaults and their assigned difficulty value at the Junior Olympic level. Some of

| VAULT NAME | LEVEL OF DIFFICULTY |
| --- | --- |
| Squat Vault | 7.0 |
| Stoop Vault | 7.5 |
| Straddle Vault | 7.5 |
| Quarter Twist On, Quarter Twist Off | 8.2 |
| Half Twist On, Repulsion Off | 8.4 |
| Handspring | 8.4 |
| Yamishita | 8.4 |
| Handspring or Yamishita On, Half Twist Off | 8.6 |
| Half On, Half Off | 8.6 |
| Quarter On, Three-Quarter Off | 8.6 |
| Half Twist On, Full Twist Off | 9.0 |
| Handspring or Yamishita On, Full Twist Off | 9.1 |

these vaults will be described later. The first three vaults listed—the squat, the stoop, and the straddle—are all beginner vaults, as we said; the rest are in the handspring family. In the two-part vaults, which are more advanced, the "on" move is performed in the preflight and the "off" move is done in the afterflight.

So that you'll know what to expect when learning to vault, let's move on now to a discussion of some examples of the vaults you will learn over time. We'll start with the most basic and progress through the more advanced.

## Squat Vault

The squat vault will probably be one of the first vaults you learn. Here's how you do it (see illustration): Run, hurdle, and rebound from the board with your body stretched practically horizontal. Place your hands on top of the horse, and bend your knees to pass over the horse in a tuck position. Push off your hands and stretch your body before landing in a demi-plié. Straighten your legs so you finish in a standing position.

Squat Vault

< 41 >

Key points to remember:
- Stretch your body to horizontal in the preflight
- Block, then rise in afterflight
- Tuck, then stretch your body upward before landing
- Stick the landing

While you are learning the squat vault, your coaches will stand to the side, between the board and the horse and between the horse and the landing mat, to help support and guide your performance through the preflight, the afterflight, and the landing. This is known as spotting.

## Handspring

This vault is the single most important skill in your development as a vaulter. Learning the handspring is the essential requirement before you can move on to advanced vaults. But it will take time to learn. Your coach will give you specialized drills so you can mas-

**Handspring**

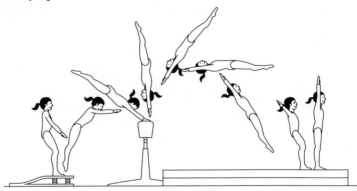

< 42 >

ter each part of the handspring before you finally per-form the entire vault without a spot.

Here's how you do it: Run, hurdle, and rebound from the board with a stretched body to an inverted (head down, legs up) position on the horse. Push off from the horse with your body stretched out, feet first, and land in a demi-plié. Then extend to stand.

Key points to remember:

• Stretch your body out in preflight, with your head held straight
• Block, then rise, heels over head, in afterflight
• Keep your body posture tight throughout
• Stick the landing

## Half On, Half Off

This is an advanced vault, with twists, from the handspring family. Here's how you do it: Run, hurdle, and rebound from the board with a stretched body. Make a half turn (180 degrees) in preflight, and reach

Half On, Half Off

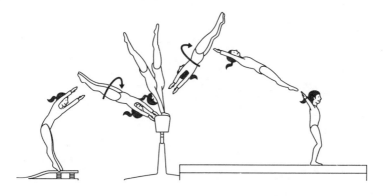

< 43 >

the horse in an inverted position. Push off from the horse with the hands, and make another half turn (180 degrees) in the afterflight to land in a demi-plié. Then extend to stand, facing away from the horse.

Key points to remember:
- Make a crisp and clean half turn in preflight
- Keep your body stretched throughout
- Make a crisp and clean half turn in afterflight
- Be in control when you land

## Tsukahara

The Tsukahara is a vault from family number 3; it is a backward salto. Mary Lou Retton performed a more advanced version of the vault we'll describe when she was awarded her perfect score of 10 at the 1984 Olympics.

Here's how you do it: Run, hurdle, and rebound from the board with a stretched body and make a half turn in the preflight to arrive on the horse in an

Tsukahara

inverted position. Push off with the hands and execute a backward one-and-a-half salto in the tuck position to land in a demi-plié. Then extend to stand. Sounds easy, right? Just kidding. Someday it will be.

Key points to remember:

- Make a crisp and clean half turn in the preflight
- Push explosively off the horse with your hands
- Go for great height in the afterflight
- Show control in landing

# How They Score It

As we mentioned earlier, the highest score that a gymnast can receive for a particular vault is the assigned difficulty rating of that vault. For example, the highest score possible for the handspring is 8.4 points. That means that everyone starts out with a perfect score. You lose points when you make any mistakes.

The judge carefully watches for errors in the performance of a vault. She is aided by a list of deductions she memorizes. For example, deductions (in fractions of a point) for the handspring vault include:

| | |
|---|---|
| Body bent in preflight | up to −0.30 |
| Legs bent straddled or opened (each) | up to −0.30 |
| Lack of repulsion | up to −1.00 |
| Insufficient height in afterflight | up to −0.50 |
| Taking one step on landing | −0.10 |
| Coach spotting between board and horse | −0.50 |

*Mary Lou Retton's vault won her the gold in 1984.*

To determine the final score, the judge adds up the special deductions she has observed, and subtracts that number from the difficulty rating of the vault. In the handspring example we just gave, if the gymnast was penalized to the full extent for each error, that would mean a total of 2.7 points deducted from the 8.4

< 46 >

difficulty rating, giving the gymnast a final score of 5.7 for the vault.

You usually will see more than one judge at a gymnastics event. In a local USGF Junior Olympic competition, there will probably be two judges. At a major event, like the Olympic Games, there might be as many as eight judges. The reason for that is to make the judging as fair as possible for each gymnast, as well as to prevent errors that might be made by a single judge.

We will talk more about judging and scoring in gymnastics as we move through the other women's events.

< 47 >

# CHAPTER 4

# UNEVEN BARS

**A**T THE 1978 WORLD CHAMPIONSHIPS in Strasbourg, France, Marcia Frederick had the opportunity to become the first American woman gymnast to win a gold medal in international competition. Marcia was the U.S. champion in the uneven bars, and she had already shown her ability to perform routines of outstanding difficulty, style, and technique.

At Strasbourg, Marcia performed well during the preliminaries and qualified for the finals. However, she drew the first-up position, which usually receives conservative scoring from judges. It would take an exceptional performance for Marcia's score to hold.

Marcia confidently performed a nearly flawless routine and stuck the landing of her pike front salto dismount over the low bar. The audience gave her a standing ovation. Although the rest of the gymnasts all demonstrated world-class routines, Marcia's routine was clearly ahead of the field. She maintained

< 48 >

*Uneven bars is hard to learn, but exciting to perform.*

her position to win the first gold medal for the U.S. in world championship competition.

# The Apparatus

The uneven bars has become one of the most exciting events in women's gymnastics. This wasn't always the case. At one time, athletes performed long, slow routines on the bars that included many stands, balances, and poses. The event has been altered, in large part thanks to changes in the design of the apparatus and in the rules.

The apparatus in the uneven bars consists of two parallel bars, or rails, at different heights from the floor. The bars are eight feet long and, more or less, round in width.

In the past, the bars were made of wood. But as gymnasts began to perform more complicated and powerful moves, the bars would sometimes break or splinter. Today, the bars are made of fiberglass and covered with a thin veneer of wood. The wood provides a nonslip gripping surface, and the fiberglass makes the bars stronger and more flexible. Together, the materials make it easier for gymnasts to perform more dramatic, high-flying skills, like release moves, in which they leave the bar to perform a move and then regrip it on their return.

The high bar is set at 92 inches (235 centimeters) off the floor and the low bar is set at 61 inches (155 cm). In international competition, the height of the two bars above the floor is the same for all gymnasts. In U.S. Junior Olympic competition, the gymnasts are allowed to change the height of the bars according to their age and height. The two uprights are separated by a spreader that allows the gymnast to select any distance between the two bars, from 23.5 inches (60 cm) to 54.5 inches (140 cm).

Just as the move from wood to fiberglass changed the event, so did the rule change that allowed gymnasts to choose the distance between the bars. Placing the uneven bars farther apart made it possible for female gymnasts to perform tricks similar to those men performed on the horizontal bar, including handstands, release moves, and giant swings, which is when the gymnast's body is completely extended during a full, 360-degree rotation around the bar.

Before the rule change, female gymnasts could not do giant swings because they didn't fit between the bars. Instead, they performed skills called beats and wraps, in which they would hit or circle the low bar with their hips. These moves are seldom seen today in international competition.

Beginning gymnasts usually set the distance between the bars fairly close, to move easily from low bar to high bar; advanced gymnasts usually select the maximum distance allowed, to perform difficult skills more easily.

The bar rails are supported by steel uprights. The tops of the uprights are connected directly to the floor (or to a steel base) by steel cables. These keep the bars

< 51 >

from moving during a performance.

The entire area under the bars is covered with landing mats to provide a secure landing for dismounts—which is the move the gymnast makes to leave the apparatus at the end of a routine—and to protect the gymnast in case she falls. Gymnasts are allowed to place a springboard on the mats to help them reach the bars at the beginning of a routine—which is known as the mount—but the board must be removed by a coach as soon as the mount is completed. That is done in case of a fall.

# The Bar Basics

The uneven bars is a difficult event to learn because it requires a strong upper body and the mastery of important lead-up skills. Developing your strength may take as long as a year. You will practice exercises like chin-ups, pull-ups, pull-overs, leg lifts, and handstand push-ups to build up your arms and shoulders.

But don't worry. Many of the first bar skills you will learn are not complicated. And they will help you develop the strength and technique you will need to progress to the complicated moves. The following are some bar building-block moves.

## Supports

A support is the starting position for most routines. In this position, you hold your body still, supported by the strength of your arms. There are, for example, the

< 52 >

front support, in which you hold the bar in front of your body, and the rear support, in which you hold the bar behind your back. The handstand would be an example of an advanced support.

## Hangs

A hang is a position in which the body is suspended under the bar. Usually, you hold yourself by the hands, but you could hang from other parts of the body, like the knees. Other examples include the long hang, the *L* hang, and the piked inverted hang.

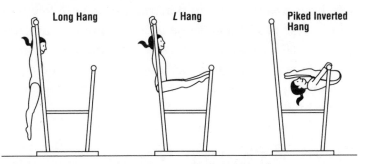

Long Hang     *L* Hang     Piked Inverted Hang

## Swings

Swings are the basic component of uneven bar skills. Basic swings include the long swing, the glide swing, and the cast.

We've all done some kind of swing, from a chinning bar or on the monkey bars, but a cast is a little more difficult. In a cast, the gymnast starts from a front support position with her hands gripped over the bar (what we call an over-grip hand-grasp). She bends her arms slightly and flexes at the hip, then swings her

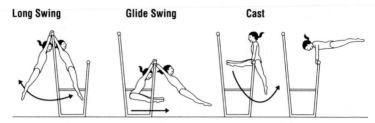

Long Swing     Glide Swing     Cast

legs backward and upward toward a handstand, keeping her body and legs perfectly straight. More advanced gymnasts are capable of reaching the handstand position.

Before your coach will let you try a cast, you'll probably have to demonstrate that you can meet a few prerequisites. You'll need to be able to complete a minimum of 10 push-ups, press to a handstand from a straddle stand on the floor, and kick to a handstand and a half pirouette on the floor. (Check the glossary if you need an explanation of these terms.)

# Some Beginner Tricks

Once you have learned all of the basic body positions and swings on the bars, the next group of skills to learn is the elementary circles. These include kickovers, pull-overs, back hip circles, front hip circles, stride circles, and sole circles.

## Back Hip Circle

The back hip includes some of the basic moves we've discussed. Here's how you do it: From a front support position on the low bar (with an over-grip

hand-grasp), cast upward to a horizontal position with straight arms, then swing downward (toward the bar) so that the hips touch the bar, while circling backward (360 degrees) until you return to the front support position.

Lead-up Work (what you'll need to be able to do before you try this move):

- A back hip pull-over to the support position
- A minimum of five pull-ups in a row
- Hang from the high bar by your hands for at least 30 seconds

Key points to remember:

- Keep your body straight on the cast
- Form a continuous circle
- Keep your arms straight during the circle
- Keep your legs straight

## Clear Hip Circle

Now, to show you how a gymnast adds on moves and progresses to advanced skills step by step, we'll give you an example of a more difficult circling skill. Here's how you do it: From a front support position in an over-grip hand-grasp, cast to above horizontal,

**Clear Hip Circle**

then swing downward from the shoulders toward the bar. Push against the bar, which will cause your shoulders to drop back and your body to circle backward around the bar in a slightly piked position without touching the bar with the hips or thighs. Advanced gymnasts are able to finish in the handstand position.

Lead-up Work:
- Backward hip circle
- Backward seat circle
- Backward sole circle
- Cast from support to near handstand

Key points to remember:
- Maintain slightly piked body position as you swing around
- Keep control of your body on the downswing
- Keep your legs straight
- Keep your arms straight throughout

## Straddle Glide Kip

A different kind of move, but one of the most important basic skills, is the straddle glide kip. A kip is a

**Straddle Glide Kip**

movement from a hanging position on a bar to a position above it, in which the body moves from an extended position into a pike and then back to an extension. Your coach will teach you the kip after you've nailed down the basic body positions and swings. It is a difficult skill for a beginner to master because it will probably be the first one you will learn that combines all the necessary body strength and coordination into one smooth movement.

Here's how you do it: From a standing position on the mat, jump from both feet and grasp the low bar in an over-grip. Swing under the bar in a piked straddle (L-shaped, legs apart) position, stretching your hips and closing your legs at the end of the swing. Lift your legs up toward the bar, and thrust open (quick extension) at the hips while pulling down on the bar with straight arms to arrive in a front support position.

Lead-up Work:
- A minimum of five pull-ups in sequence
- Back hip pull-over to front support position
- A minimum of eight straight leg lifts in a row

Key points to remember:
- Extend the glide, or swing, as far as you can
- Swing with full amplitude (that means the most

complete extension of the body)

- Keep your legs straight
- Keep your arms straight throughout

## Straddle Sole Circle Dismount

Here's how you do it: From a straddle stand on the low bar, with the hands on the high bar, reach downward to grasp the low bar between the feet in an overgrip. Execute a three-quarter backward sole circle with straight legs. As the feet leave the bar, extend the legs while opening the body to dismount to a landing in a demi-plié, then extend to stand.

Key points to remember:

- Keep legs straight
- Bring legs together in flight from bar
- Show height and distance in flight from the bar
- Land in demi-plié

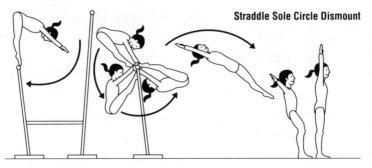

Straddle Sole Circle Dismount

# Conditioning and Confidence

Until you have developed sufficient strength, your coach will have to help you practice hundreds of kips.

< 58 >

But one day, you will come into the gym and approach the bar event and discover that you can do a kip all by yourself! It will seem so easy that you will wonder why it took so long.

You will find that the pattern of learning the kip is similar to learning other important skills, like the cast to handstand and the giant swing. There will be a period of time when it will seem as if you will never get it. But during this period, your body is actually gaining the strength and coordination it needs to perform the skill. Once your body is ready, the skill will come quickly and easily.

Becoming a good uneven bar performer requires patience and lots of hard work on your conditioning program. Those who stay with it find that the uneven bars becomes one of their favorite events.

# What Goes into a Bar Routine

Uneven bar routines usually contain 10 to 12 different tricks, or elements. Each element has a difficulty rating. *A* elements are the basic skills, and they are considered easy; *B* elements are of intermediate difficulty; *C* elements are more difficult; and *D* elements are the hardest of all. The chart on the next page shows how some typical bar tricks are rated for difficulty.

In an uneven-bar routine, the gymnast moves back and forth from one rail to the other while executing a series of kips, swings, circles, and saltos, continuously,

| DIFFICULTY | ELEMENT |
| --- | --- |
| **A** | Glide kip<br>Clear hip circle to front support |
| **B** | Clear hip circle to a handstand position<br>Cast to handstand with legs together and hips extended |
| **C** | Giant swing on the high bar<br>Flyaway double back dismount in tuck position (after releasing the bar with her hands, the gymnast does two backward saltos in a tuck position, then lands onto the mat) |
| **D** | Handstand with a full turn (full pirouette)<br>Flyaway double back dismount in layout position (after releasing, the gymnast does two backward saltos with the body straight) |

from start to finish. Except for the briefest moments, the gymnast must support her entire weight from her hands throughout the routine. The routine must include movements both on the low bar and on the high bar. In her routine, the gymnast will use many grip changes, releases, and regrasps, flying-type elements, changes of direction, and handstands.

Only five elements in a row may be performed on the same bar. The routine should flow from one movement to the next without pauses, extra swings, or additional supports. Although there is no required time limit, it usually takes about 50 seconds to perform the minimum of 10 elements in a routine.

< **60** >

# Compulsories and Optionals

In compulsory routines, gymnasts compete by performing the same required skills. The other kind of routine is the optional routine. In an optional, the gymnast can choose the skills she wants to include, the style, and even the length of her program.

The USGF Junior Olympic women's program is divided into 10 levels. The first four levels are for teaching basic gymnastics skills to beginner gymnasts. Levels 5-10 are the competitive levels; level 5 is considered the beginner competitive level, and level 10 the advanced level. In levels 5-7, the gymnasts compete using the required compulsory routines. At levels 8 and 9, you are permitted to compete using your own routines. At level 10, the gymnasts compete in two sets of routines—compulsories and optionals. Gymnasts are allowed to advance to a higher level only after they have shown skill and received good scores at their current level.

# Sore Hands and Handgrips

As your training on the bars increases, your hands will become red and sore; you might even have a rip (a blister that tears open). This is common among new gymnasts; eventually, your hands will build a protective layer of callouses.

To protect their hands and get a secure grip on the bar, many gymnasts use handgrips. Handgrips are

< 61 >

*Marcia Frederick was a world champion on the bars.*

usually made of leather, lampwick, or tape.

When you are ready for your first pair of grips, ask your coach to help you select the correct size and teach you how to use and care for them properly. It is important that handgrips be broken in before you try them out and that you first use them while practicing basic skills. This breaking-in time allows you to work some of the stiffness out of the grips and get used to the feel of the apparatus through them before moving on to newer skills.

# How They Score It

The job of scoring an uneven-bar routine is not easy. A judge must evaluate the following factors:

• **Difficulty.** She must keep track of all the elements a gymnast performs and know the difficulty value assigned to each element.

• **Composition.** A gymnast has certain requirements in her routine, such as a minimum of 10 elements. If anything is missing, the judge will make a deduction.

• **Execution.** This category refers to how a gymnast performs each element. For example, the judge could make the following deductions (in fractions of a point) when a gymnast performs a straddle glide kip:

| | |
|---|---|
| Incomplete extension of glide | up to −0.20 |
| Insufficient amplitude (swing) to kip | up to −0.20 |
| Excessive arm bend | up to −0.30 |
| Legs bent during glide | up to −0.30 |

At the end of the routine, the judge adds up all of her deductions for the three categories and subtracts this total from 10 points to determine the gymnast's final score. A score of 10 is a perfect score, since the judge made no deductions in any of the categories.

Like the other events, the uneven bars event is usually scored by at least two judges. When two judges are used, their scores are averaged. If one judge's score for a routine is 8.2 and the other judge's score is 8.4, a gymnast's final score would be 8.3.

# CHAPTER 5

# BALANCE BEAM

**Y**OU MAY REMEMBER CATHY RIGBY as the star of the musical Peter Pan, which toured all over the country and then played on Broadway. Before she became an actress, Cathy was a commentator for ABC Sports. But before that, Cathy had been an outstanding gymnast. She was a member of the U.S. Olympic team in 1968 and 1972.

Cathy became the first modern-era gymnast from the U.S. to win a medal in international competition when she received the silver in the balance beam event at the 1970 world championships in Ljubljana [*leh-OOH-bleh-AYN-eh*], Yugoslavia.

Known as a consistent and rock-steady beam performer, Cathy competed at a time when gymnasts were beginning to include more gymnastics (or tumbling) skills in their routines. Cathy's championship routine included a flic-flac, a press to stag-handstand, and a front aerial dismount. What are those? Read on,

< 64 >

*On the beam, a gymnast's stage is but four inches wide.*

and you'll find out all about the balance beam event.

# On the Beam

The balance beam is a long, narrow piece of wood or metal, topped with a foam pad and tightly covered with a nonskid material, usually suede leather or a synthetic fabric. The beam measures 4 inches wide by 16 feet long, and rests on an adjustable steel base.

In the past, balance beams were constructed entirely of wood. The padded beam we use today is softer and less slippery. This allows gymnasts to perform complicated tumbling and acrobatic maneuvers that were not possible before.

The standard height of the balance beam for the Olympics and international competition is four feet (120 cm) off the floor. But as with vaulting and uneven bars, the height of the balance beam may be lowered for the younger, less experienced gymnast. In fact, the acceptable heights for the balance beam in Junior Olympic competitions are the same as for vaulting. That is, 45.25 inches for the junior division (ages 12-14) and 43.25 for the children's division (ages 9-11).

Landing mats are placed at each end of the balance beam and on both sides of the beam. Together, they form a safety zone in case the gymnast should fall. As in the uneven bars, gymnasts can place a springboard on the mats for mounting the beam at the beginning of a routine, but the board must be removed by a coach as soon as the mount has been made.

< 66 >

# Learning Balance and More

Each of the events that we've talked about so far makes its own demands upon the gymnast. Vaulting requires speed, power, and courage. Uneven bars demand great upper-body strength, power, flexibility, and coordination. You might guess that balance is critical in the balance beam event. But the good beam performer also must have great flexibility, grace, rhythm, tumbling ability, confidence, and concentration.

In the balance beam, the gymnast performs a combination of dance skills, basic locomotor movements (runs, hops, and skips), and tumbling tricks. (We'll talk more about tumbling in chapter seven.)

To learn how to perform on the beam, you must be patient enough to master each skill in turn. As we explained in chapter two, this process is called learning by progressions. Progressions are used to teach skills for all of the gymnastics events, but they are most important in teaching the beam. Otherwise, it could be a little scary to perform moves on a four-inch wide beam that is raised four feet above the ground.

The first time you are introduced to a new skill for the beam, you will learn it on mats on the floor. Then, you will learn to perform the skill on a straight line on the floor. Once you have mastered these, you will move the skill to a beam that sits right on the floor. Your coach might use what we call a beam pad to widen and soften the surface. (A beam pad is a one-inch-thick vinyl mat that fits around the beam.)

< 67 >

As you become more comfortable on the beam, you will move to higher and higher beams—first with extra padding, and then with the pads removed. That way, by the time you are ready to perform the skill on the high beam, you will have complete confidence in your ability.

Because of the height of the beam, falls become a little more dangerous—and you *will* fall when learning the beam! It is very important that as you learn a new skill, you learn how to fall properly. The landing drills you learn in vaulting will be helpful. On the beam, when in doubt, use additional mats or ask your coach for a spot.

# Body Alignment Training

The key to becoming a good balance-beam performer is learning to maintain good body position while you are balancing yourself or moving across the beam. Good body position in gymnastics is the same as good posture in everyday life; that means keeping your back straight, your head aligned with your spine, and your body balanced on both sides. Dance and ballet training are very helpful in developing correct posture, which will enable you to maintain alignment and keep your center of gravity over the beam.

You can also develop this ability by practicing drills, such as the beam complex warm-up. This is an excellent warm-up, as well as a good flexibility and alignment exercise. The complex begins with very simple movements up and down the beam—walks, runs, skips, and hops. Gradually, the movements become more complicated and demanding, with leaps and turns testing the gymnast's balance.

The value of this training is that it keeps the gymnast constantly working to improve and maintain correct body position until it becomes automatic. From beginner to Olympian, all gymnasts work on similar alignment drills every day.

# Balancing Acts

The second part of balance beam training is learning the gymnastics moves that must be mastered to perfection. These include all of the tricks—cartwheels, walkovers, flic-flacs, mounts, and dismounts. On the following pages, we'll give you examples and talk you through the movements.

## Squat on Mount

Here's how you do it: Place the springboard at a right angle to the beam. Begin in a stand facing the beam. From a running start of two or three steps, or from a standing position on the board, take off with both feet in the air, and place both hands on top of the beam. Lift your hips high and quickly bend at the knees to place both feet between your hands on the beam in a squat position. Stand up, rise to a relevé position (on the balls of your feet), and turn 90 degrees to face the end of the beam. From there, you

< 69 >

will begin your routine.

Key points to remember:

- Strong push with the arms
- Good height of hips above the beam
- Keep your toes pointed on the way up
- Control where you place your feet on the beam

## Straight Jump Traveling Forward

Step forward onto your right leg. Place the ball of the left foot behind the right foot in a demi-plié and jump into the air, traveling forward and stretching your body. As you jump, your arms are lifted high above the head and then moved downward, forward, and upward to vertical. Land in a demi-plié, and step forward onto a straight right leg. Keep your left leg extended backward, with toes pointed on the beam. Lower your arms to the side middle position.

Key points to remember:

- Stand in demi-plié for takeoff
- Stretch out fully during the jump

**Straight Jump**

- Show good distance and height in the jump
- Hold the demi-plié on landing

## Forward Roll

The roll begins with you facing the end of the beam, with your feet together in a squat position. The hands are placed a comfortable distance from the feet, side-by-side with the thumbs on top of the beam. Lift the hips high enough for the head to be completely tucked under the body and between the hands. After the head has been tucked, straighten the legs and let the elbows squeeze the head. Roll through a squat position to walk out to a stand on one foot, then the other foot. Finish standing with the weight on the forward leg and the rear leg stretched behind.

Key points to remember:

- Keep hands on top of the beam throughout roll
- Be sure the roll is continuous and smooth

**Forward Roll**

- Maintain good form
- Finish in a standing position

To spot this skill, the coach will stand alongside the beam, to the side but slightly in front of the gymnast. As the gymnast tucks her head under, the spotter will grasp her hips and guide them along the beam. The spotter will then help the gymnast from a squat into a standing position. Beam pads come in handy in practicing this skill. They can be placed on the beam to protect the gymnast's back.

## Back Walkover

You will probably spend a lot of time practicing this skill on a straight line on the floor before you move up to the beam. To do a good back walkover, your body alignment must be excellent.

Here's how it's done: Facing the end of the beam, stand on one foot that is slightly turned out. Extend your free leg forward, slightly turned out with pointed toes. There should be no weight on this foot. The arms are extended straight above the head. The head is neutral (neither tilted forward nor backward) and remains that way throughout the trick.

Begin the back walkover with a large upward and backward stretch of the shoulders. This stretch will be

continued until your hands reach the beam, and it will cause your back to arch. Try to find the beam with your eyes, without tilting your head. As you stretch your arms, lift your forward leg. Continue doing both until your hands reach the beam. Then push off from the foot of your support leg so that you arrive in a handstand position with legs split. Ideally, you should show a complete, 180-degree split in the handstand to receive no deductions from the judges. If you can't do that, at least try to keep the legs evenly balanced.

Your hands should be together and your back should be straight, in the handstand position. Step down to a stand with the forward leg bent and the backward leg extended (this is the lunge position) to finish the walkover.

Key points to remember:
• Maintain good alignment and body position
• Go for a full split, or at least a balanced one
• Stay in control while in the handstand position
• Finish in a lunge position with good alignment

## 360-Degree Turn on One Leg

From a stand on a straight left leg, step forward with your right foot. Demi-plié into a lunge, extending

the left leg backward and placing the left foot flat across the width of the beam. Holding your arms above your head with slightly bent elbows (which is called the crown position), shift your weight forward, and extend your right leg to execute a 360-degree turn to the right on the ball of the right foot (this is called a relevé). As the turn begins, move your left leg from the rear to a 45-degree downward angle. After 90 degrees of turn, bend the left leg at the knee to touch the toes to the right ankle (the passé position). Finish the turn in control over the supporting leg.

Key points to remember:
- Maintain good posture throughout the turn
- Complete the full 360 degrees of rotation
- Execute the turn high on the ball of the right foot
- Show you're in control at the finish

## Roundoff Dismount

A roundoff is a cartwheel that allows the gymnast to turn 180 degrees and finish off facing the direction from which she came. (For an illustration of a cartwheel, see chapter six.) And a dismount is the move-

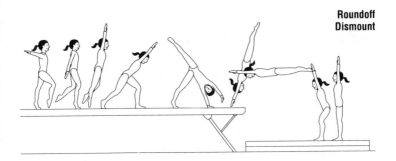

ment that lets you leave the apparatus and end your routine.

Here's how you do it: Start standing on a straight right leg, with your left leg straight and pointed forward on the beam. From running steps, with or without a hurdle, execute the roundoff cartwheel so that you have turned 180 degrees while passing through the handstand position as you reach the end of the beam. Dismount in a stretched body position with a strong push from the hands. Land in a cross-stand, facing the end of the beam. Bend the knees in a demi-plié, and extend to stand.

Key points to remember:

- Keep your legs straight through the roundoff
- Push strongly from both hands on the dismount
- Maintain a stretched-out body position in flight
- Land in a demi-plié

# Putting It All Together

As we explained in chapter four, beginning gymnasts perform compulsory routines in their first levels of competition. Later on, they move to optional routines. In competition, the optional balance beam routine lasts between 70 and 90 seconds and must cover the entire length of the beam. In creating your routine, you and your coach will use acrobatic, gymnastics, and dance movements to create high points, or dramatic peaks, in the exercise. The routine must contain a mount and a dismount that are of equal difficulty to the rest of the routine.

Your routine should include leaps and jumps, both as single elements and in series. These are called the gymnastics elements. An example of a gymnastics series is a balance into a body wave into a turn, followed by a split leap.

A turn on one leg of at least 360 degrees is required. You will also want to include tumbling skills. These are called acrobatic elements and include walkovers, cartwheels, and flic-flacs (back handsprings). All of the skill elements are connected through dance movements and poses.

As in uneven bars and floor exercise, each element you perform on the beam is rated for level of difficulty at A, B, C, or D. The rules usually require a minimum number of skills performed at each level. For example, in international competition the gymnasts must perform at least one A, two B's, two C's, and one D. If the judge determines that the gymnast did not include the required number of difficulties, she will make a deduction in the gymnast's score.

To give you an idea how this works, following are

some balance beam tricks (some we've talked about, some more advanced) and their difficulty ratings.

| DIFFICULTY | ELEMENT |
| --- | --- |
| A | Split leap<br>Cartwheel |
| B | Flic-flac (back handspring)<br>Roundoff on the beam (not a dismount) |
| C | Layout salto backward with step-out on the beam (usually performed in series from a roundoff or flic-flac)<br>Aerial cartwheel (a cartwheel without the hands touching the beam) |
| D | Backward salto with a full twist on the beam (This one is really difficult!)<br>Double back salto dismount (usually performed in series from a roundoff or roundoff, flic-flac combination) |

# How They Score It

The balance beam event is scored in the same way as the uneven bars and the floor exercise. The judge takes deductions in the categories of difficulty, composition, and execution, and subtracts them from the highest possible score of 10 points.

What happens if I fall off the beam on my back walkover during my routine? If you completed your walkover and then fell off, the judge will deduct 0.5 point from your score. You must remount the beam

< 77 >

*Cathy Rigby made history when she won the silver medal in the balance beam at the 1970 world championships.*

and continue your routine within 10 seconds, or you will receive an additional deduction. If you fell off the beam before you completed your back walkover, the judge will deduct 0.5 point for the fall and will not give you difficulty credit for the element.

Because balance beam is a timed event, the judges

< 78 >

have special deductions if your routine is too short or too long. If your routine was too short (less than 70 seconds), the judge will deduct 0.20 from your final score. If the routine was too long (longer than 90 seconds), the judge will deduct 0.20 from your final score. You do get some help here, though. Ten seconds before the time limit, the judge rings a warning bell—that means you better get ready for your dismount right away!

Sometimes, in a state meet or the national championships, there are four judges. How is the gymnast's final score determined in this case? Each judge awards her own score, and the final score is determined by dropping the highest score and the lowest score and averaging the two middle scores.

The judges watch for variations in rhythm, changes in levels (from sitting on the beam to sailing head-height above it), and the harmonious blend of gymnastics and acrobatic elements. The overall execution of your routine should give the impression that you are performing on a floor 40 feet wide, not on a narrow, 4-inch strip.

Speaking of a 40-foot wide floor, we are just about ready for your last event: the floor exercise.

# CHAPTER 6

# FLOOR EXERCISE

**W**E'VE TALKED A LOT ABOUT judging and scoring in gymnastics events and how different judges sometimes see (and score) performances differently. The floor exercise is particularly difficult to score because it combines many types of movements. Sometimes judges can even be influenced by a gymnast's reputation without realizing it. But whatever the scoring of one particular routine, hard work and dedication always pay off.

At the 1978 world championships in Strasbourg, France, Kathy Johnson of the United States had the tough luck to have to follow the great Nadia Comaneci of Romania in every event of the individual all-around competition. Just two years earlier, at the 1976 Olympics, Nadia had won gold medals in the all-around, the balance beam, and the uneven bars, a silver in the team competition, and a bronze in the floor exercise. She had also become the first gymnast ever

< 80 >

*The floor is a good place for a beginner to start.*

< 81 >

to receive a perfect score in Olympic competition. The judges at the world championships were well aware of Nadia's reputation.

In the floor exercise at Strasbourg, Nadia performed a solid routine and received a score of 9.80. Then it was Kathy's turn. Kathy's routine was classically elegant, artistic, and even more difficult than Nadia's. When the judges flashed a score of only 9.75 for Kathy, the audience broke into loud whistles of protest that lasted for nearly 10 minutes. The U.S. coaches submitted a protest, and Kathy's score was adjusted upward to 9.90. Later, in the finals of the floor exercise competition, Kathy won the silver medal in a tie with Emilia Eberle of Romania.

Kathy was a fine all-around gymnast herself. In 1984, as a member of the U.S. Olympic squad that won the silver medal as a team, Kathy earned a bronze in balance beam and placed 10th in the all-around. Like Cathy Rigby, Kathy Johnson became a television sports commentator after retiring from competitive gymnastics.

# A View from the Floor

The floor exercise is performed on a mat or a special floor known as a spring floor—a springy, yet firm, surface that enables the gymnast to do her most high-flying and dramatic tricks and still land safely.

In the early days of gymnastics, floor-exercise routines were performed on a wooden floor. As the sport

< 82 >

evolved, gymnasts were permitted to place mats within the floor area for tumbling maneuvers. Eventually, the entire area was covered with matting.

The spring floor used today is built from plywood sheets and a layer of rubber, foam, or springs. It is topped with a soft elastic material, such as rubber, and covered with a carpet or carpetlike material.

The floor measures 40 feet square. The performance area is surrounded by a 2-foot border, in case the gymnast should step or fall out of bounds.

The gymnast must perform her entire routine within the marked boundaries of the floor. If she steps or falls out of this area, she will receive a deduction from the judges. In national and international competitions, there are two line judges who do nothing but watch for these errors. If the gymnast goes beyond the boundaries even by a fraction of an inch, the nearest line judge will raise a yellow flag to inform the scoring judges that an error has been made.

# Beginner's Favorite

The floor exercise is perhaps the most dramatic and beautiful of the women's competitive events. It combines movements from tumbling, dance (classical, modern, and popular), and rhythmic gymnastics in a routine that lasts from 70 to 90 seconds and is performed to music.

Floor exercise is a favorite among young gymnasts. It is usually easier for a beginnner to get started with

< 83 >

a floor routine than it is to learn the first routines on the balance beam or uneven bars. As one young gymnast said, "It is pretty hard to fall off the floor!"

You might think that the floor would be an easy event, but, actually, it is very demanding. That's because the floor requires each gymnast to master a great number of difficult skills. And even some of the basic skills require time and effort to learn to perform with precision and amplitude.

# The Acrobatic Side

Gymnasts use the term acrobatic movements to refer to what most of us know as tumbling skills. These include cartwheels, handsprings, and saltos.

You will learn a wide variety of acrobatic movements for your floor-exercise routine. These may be performed alone, in a series, or in a combination with the gymnastics elements (which we will talk about later). A series is a group of movements that are directly connected to one another without stops or unnecessary steps. Most floor-exercise routines contain three major tumbling series of three to five moves each. In international competition, high-level athletes may show as many as five different tumbling runs.

In your tumbling series, you will learn to perform both forward and backward wheels, springs, and saltos. The first tumbling series performed in a routine is called the mount, even though you are already on the floor. The final acrobatic series is called the dis-

< 84 >

mount, even though you don't actually leave the floor.

Just as with the other competitive events, each acrobatic element in a floor routine has an assigned difficulty rating. Some examples are:

| DIFFICULTY | ELEMENT |
|---|---|
| A | Cartwheels (including an aerial cartwheel) |
| | Flic-flacs |
| | Basic saltos (in tuck, pike, and layout positions) |
| B | Brani (front salto with half twist) |
| | Backward salto with full twist |
| | Arabian salto |
| C | Backward salto with double twist |
| D | Backward double salto (layout) |
| | Backward double salto (tuck position) |
| | Backward salto with triple twist |

Here's how some of those movements look when they're put into typical acrobatic series in a beginner's competitive routine.

1. Roundoff, flic-flac, flic-flac
2. Front salto step-out, front handspring, dive-roll
3. Roundoff, flic-flac, flic-flac, back salto (layout)

As you can see, a gymnast must be a very accomplished tumbler to perform the acrobatic elements at the higher levels of difficulty. However, since tumbling is so much fun, and your coach teaches you by using progressions, it won't be long before you will have mastered the basics. Then you will be able to move on

< 85 >

to the more difficult tumbling skills. As we've said before, progressions are the way to learn all gymnastics skills safely and efficiently.

# The Gymnastics Side

In the floor exercise, we use the term gymnastics elements to refer to skills from dance and rhythmic gymnastics that have been singled out and given difficulty ratings. These include leaps, turns, and jumps. Here are some examples of gymnastics movements and their levels of difficulty:

| DIFFICULTY | ELEMENT |
| --- | --- |
| A | Handstands |
| | Basic leaps, jumps, hops, turns (pirouettes), and locomotor movements |
| B | Leaps with amplitude (for example, those that show a full 180-degree split of the legs) |
| | Jumps with amplitude (for example, straddle jump with full 180-degree split) |
| | Handstands with at least one and a half pirouettes |
| C | Double turn on one leg |
| | Switch-split leap with half turn |
| D | Triple turn on one leg |

## Turn Up the Amplitude

To receive credit from the judges for performing these gymnastics elements, you must do them precise-

< 86 >

ly and show good amplitude. What is amplitude? Amplitude is the way you use your body to perform a routine, whether it's getting great height off the floor or extending yourself to the limit in a body stretch. Amplitude is important in all gymnastics elements.

Gymnasts who get greater height off the ground when performing a leap or a salto show greater amplitude. Likewise, gymnasts can demonstrate differences in what we call internal amplitude in the degree of leg stretch during a split leap or the height of a held leg in an arabesque position.

In their scoring of the floor exercise, judges will make a deduction in the execution category for an element that is performed with poor amplitude. Or they might devalue the difficulty level of the skill based upon the amplitude of a gymnast's performance. For example, a switch split leap (a split of the legs followed by a switching of the legs in the air and a split on the other leg) that shows a 180-degree angle of the legs will receive a *B* difficulty rating, but if the gymnast performs the same leap with less than a 135-degree angle of the legs, she will receive an *A* difficulty credit.

## Getting That Extra Edge

Unless you are gifted with natural flexibility, you will need many hours of practice in the gym and in the dance room to develop precision and amplitude. But the good news is that these qualities *can* be developed if you are willing to devote the time and energy to your flexibility and strength training.

< 87 >

Since floor exercise combines the elements of tumbling and dance, many gymnastics programs offer a separate dance class or devote part of the tumbling or warm-up periods to work on these important elements. If your club doesn't offer separate dance training, you might want to consider enrolling in a good ballet class.

# Skills and Progressions

The tumbling skills that you learn in floor exercise will help you greatly in the other events. In general, you will learn a skill first on the floor, and then on the other equipment.

Think of handstands, for example. The handstand is a basic position that is used in all of the events. Even though you don't hold the handstand for one to three seconds while doing a vault, you must pass through the handstand position on most vaults. Another example is the back extension to a handstand on the floor. If you learn to perform this with straight arms, you will find it easier to learn the clear hip circle to a handstand on the bars, which is similar.

Therefore, it is important you develop your tumbling skills in an orderly and progressive manner, paying particular attention to the basics. You need to focus on the big picture. Every skill you learn in tumbling will help you learn more difficult skills, both in tumbling and in other events. Don't take shortcuts just to learn a skill for its own sake; take the time and

< 88 >

the extra effort to learn the skill correctly. This will help you in the long run.

There are two ways of learning any skill: the one that is fastest and easiest for now and the one that is slower but will be more helpful in the long run. Gymnastics is basically a collection of different skills combined in many different ways. Everything you learn, no matter how minor it seems, will lead to something else, all of which will be used later in developing your routines. So don't skimp or get lazy about the basics, because you will need them later on. Take the time to learn to do them right the first time.

# Basic Tumbling Skills

## Handstand

The handstand is, perhaps, the most important move in gymnastics, and significant time should be spent on perfecting it. Before you start, you should be able to do a good forward roll so you can easily recover from a fall while learning the handstand.

Here's how you do it: Step forward into a lunge. While pushing from your front foot, kick your rear leg upward and backward to a handstand, with legs together. Hold the handstand for one second. Step down through an arabesque to a lunge. Return to the basic stretched stand.

Key points to remember:
• Keep body alignment when reaching for floor

**Handstand**

- Keep arms and body straight in the handstand
- Hold the handstand for one second
- Pass through the arabesque position to step down

Turns in the handstand position are called pirouettes. A half turn would be called a half pirouette, a full turn would be called a full pirouette. To perform a pirouette, the gymnast actually picks up her hands one at a time while they are supporting her body weight and "walks" them around, just as she would do with her feet on the floor when turning.

## Backward Extension Roll

The backward extension roll combines the basic backward roll in a tuck position with a shoot to a handstand. Here's how you do it: Bend the knees and begin a backward roll in the tuck position. Keeping your head tucked forward, place your hands on the floor behind your head. As your legs pass over your

**Backward Extension Roll**

< 90 >

head, extend your hips, knees, and arms to reach the handstand position. Step down to a lunge and close to a basic stretched stand.

Key points to remember:
- Stretch out your body in the handstand
- In tuck roll, be sure movements are over the top
- Keep your legs together
- Control the step-down

## Cartwheel Right

Step sideward through a right sideward lunge. Cartwheel right by placing the hands alternately on the floor (right, then left). Continue the motion of the wheel, with the legs in the straddle position, as the body passes through a handstand. Step down sideward through a left lunge by landing first on the left foot, then on the right, maintaining a sideward position throughout.

Key points to remember:
- Maintain an even rhythm in the placement of the hands and then the feet on the floor
- Stretch out your body
- Be sure arms and legs are held straight

Cartwheel Right

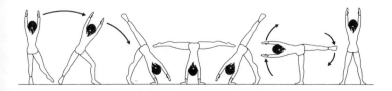

< 91 >

- Make sure the body remains sideways throughout and that the wheel motion is in a straight line

## Front Handspring Step-Out

From two or three running steps, hurdle and launch into a front handspring by reaching forward to the floor with both hands. Your rear leg should kick backward and upward vigorously. As your body passes through the handstand, push strongly from the arms and shoulders to continue the forward rotation of the body with flight. The legs remain split throughout the execution of the handspring. Land on one leg, extend the other forward. Step forward and close feet to a basic stand.

Key points to remember:
- Push strongly from the hands
- Stretch out your body in flight
- Keep arms and legs straight
- Execute a controlled landing on one foot

**Front Handspring Step-Out**

## Flic–Flac Rebound

Bend your knees and jump backward onto your hands through a stretched body position in the air. As the body passes through the handstand position, push

**Flic-Flac Rebound**

vigorously from the arms and shoulders to continue the backward rotation with flight to land on two feet and rebound with a stretched body. Land on both feet.

Key points to remember:
- Keep arms and legs straight
- Body should be stretched during flic-flac
- Push strongly from the hands
- Body should be stretched on rebound

# Shall We Dance?

Gymnastics borrows many elements and terminology from dance. Gymnasts take only what they can easily work into their routines. Included below are some of the common dance elements that gymnasts perform on both the floor and the balance beam.

## Five Positions of the Feet

There are five positions of the feet in dance, but gymnastics skills tend to be performed only in the first and second positions. In first position, the gymnast stands with heels touching and toes turned outward; to get into second position, the right leg is extended sideward so that the heels are between seven and nine inches apart, depending upon the size of the gymnast.

## Split

The split is an important position in gymnastics and is performed on the floor, beam, and occasionally at the bars. Gymnasts should develop a full 180-degree split of the legs in three positions: right leg split, left leg split, and center split.

Split

## 360-Degree Turn

Turn possibilities are virtually endless because the gymnast has a choice of different leg and arm positions, as well as direction of turn (right or left), support leg (right or left) and even the height of the turn. In gymnastics, turns are performed on the floor and on the beam. For an illustration and description of a turn, turn to chapter five.

## Split Leap

Here's how you do it: Take two running steps for-

< 94 >

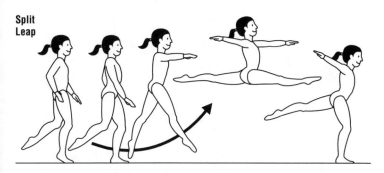

Split Leap

ward—right, left—then leap with right leg extended forward, rear leg extended backward to form a 180-degree angle in flight. Land on the right leg, demi-plié. The left leg is stretched backward and upward.

Key points to remember:
- Show good height
- Show sufficient split of the legs
- Maintain good body position
- Demi-plié on landing

There are many varieties of the split leap. For example, in a stag leap, the front leg is bent at the knee and the back leg is stretched; in a double stag leap, both legs are bent at the knee. Then there is a switch leap, a description of which follows.

## Switch Leap

Run two or three steps with a counter swing of the arms. Execute a split leap forward. At the top of the leap, quickly change the legs by scissoring them beneath the body to show a second split in flight. Land in a demi-plié on the forward leg with the rear leg stretched behind.

< 95 >

Key points to remember:
• Show good height
• Show sufficient split of the legs (130 degrees on the first leg position, 180 degrees on the second)
• Maintain a good general rhythm
• Demi-plié on landing

# Putting It All Together

What makes floor exercise so exciting is that throughout her program, the gymnast must blend all of the different elements that go into this event while using all of the floor space available to her. She is always changing the direction and the level of movement; sometimes she is in the air, sometimes on the mat. She is striving to create peaks of excitement in her program.

In addition to tumbling and dance elements, floor exercise also draws on some of the skills of another form of gymnastics: rhythmic gymnastics. We will discuss that in our next chapter.

*Kathy Johnson of the U.S. won the silver medal in the floor exercise at the 1978 world championships.*

< 97 >

# CHAPTER 7

# RHYTHMIC GYMNASTICS

**M**ANY YOUNG GIRLS DREAM of becoming an Olympic gymnast. One such dreamer was Diane Simpson from Evanston, Illinois. Diane started taking classes in rhythmic gymnastics when she was 13 years old. She worked very hard, and finally made it to the national championships three years later. But she finished in 47th place!

The next year, Diane worked even harder in the gym. At the national championships, she moved up to 21st place. Three more years of hard work and three more national championships followed. Diane finished in third place one year and second place the next two. Finally, in 1988, after six years of training, Diane won the highest honor: She became the U.S. national rhythmic gymnastics champion, and she made the U.S. Olympic Team.

Diane competed well at the Olympic Games in Seoul, South Korea, but she didn't win a medal. She

*Rhythmic gymnasts use handheld apparatus, like a hoop.*

< 99 >

didn't even make the finals. But that didn't discourage her. "I was able to compete in the greatest sporting event that exists—the Olympic Games...my lifetime dream," she says.

Diane is still training today. Her goal is to make the 1992 U.S. Olympic Team—and this time win a medal.

# The New Kid on the Block

While artistic gymnasts work on heavy fixed equipment, rhythmic gymnasts perform their skills using light handheld apparatus. These are the rope, hoop, ball, clubs, and ribbon.

Although rhythmic gymnastics (or rhythmic sportive gymnastics, as it is more formally known) is relatively new as an Olympic sport, it has been around in one form or another for as long as artistic gymnastics has—which is about as long as people have been exercising. Using light handheld apparatus in exercise programs was especially popular in Europe in the late 18th and 19th centuries. If you look through old gymnastics books, you will see pictures of people using Indian clubs, small dumbbells, hoops, and balls while doing exercise movements.

No one knows exactly when, but the story goes that in the early 1900's exercise classes began doing these exercises to music to keep all of the participants in the class moving together. That's how it came to be called rhythmic gymnastics.

Over the years, these rhythmic exercises evolved

< 100 >

into rhythmic gymnastics routines done specifically by girls to help them become more graceful. Women's artistic gymnastics teams practiced rhythmic gymnastics routines in the 1940's and 1950's as part of their training. In fact, female gymnasts performed a rhythmic gymnastics routine as the fifth event in their competitions, along with the balance beam, vault, uneven bars, and floor exercise. However, after the 1956 Olympic Games, it was decided that the five events were too much for the women to practice. Rhythmic gymnastics was removed from the Olympic program.

The women who practiced rhythmic gymnastics then decided to make it a separate sport. Between 1956 and 1963, the development of rhythmic gymnastics on its own made great progress in the Soviet Union and in other Eastern European countries. In 1961, the first international rhythmic gymnastics competition was held in Bulgaria. Following that meet, in 1962, the Federation of International Gymnastics officially recognized rhythmic gymnastics as an independent sport. The first rhythmic world championship was held in 1963.

European coaches who had immigrated to the United States began to teach the sport here. In 1973, the first rhythmic gymnastics national championship was held in the U.S. Finally, in 1984, rhythmic gymnastics made its first appearance as a medal sport at the Summer Olympics in Los Angeles, California. Today, the sport is taught in more than 50 countries around the world.

< 101 >

# What Is Rhythmic Gymnastics?

Girls who love music and dance, enjoy being creative, and who are looking for a new challenge will find rhythmic gymnastics a fun sport.

When a girl first enrolls in a rhythmic gymnastics class, she will learn the basic skills for each piece of equipment used in the sport. For example, basic skills that are performed with the rope are jumping, tossing and catching, and skipping. Once a gymnast has mastered these skills, she will learn to add basic ballet steps, like turns and leaps, while she is tossing and catching the rope. Finally, she will be taught how to put all of these skills together to music.

Below are examples of the beginning level skills that a rhythmic gymnast will practice with each piece of rhythmic equipment.

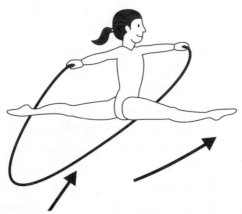

This gymnast is doing a split leap over a turning rope. To perform this skill well, a gymnast must leap high into the air and coordinate the rope turn with her jump.

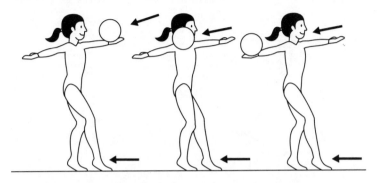

The girl in this picture is rolling the ball from her left hand to her right hand across her chest. During this movement the ball must roll smoothly along the length of both arms.

In this skill, the gymnast rolls the hoop along the ground, then takes several running steps and does a tuck jump over the rolling hoop. In order to perform this without touching the hoop, the gymnast must jump high into the air.

Rhythmic gymnasts always use two clubs at a time.

This gymnast is performing a stag jump and tossing one club in the air while making a circle with the other.

This gymnast is performing a full turn while she is making snakes with the ribbon. The arm and wrist

must move very fast in order to keep the ribbon going in a snakelike shape.

< 104 >

# Try It at Home

One of the great things about rhythmic gymnastics is that the beginner can use equipment easily found in most toy stores. Gymnasts who compete at the higher levels must use regulation equipment. But to get started all you need is a jump rope, a ball, and a hoop (many girls at first use hula-hoops). Girls can make their own ribbons by buying a long piece of satin ribbon and tying it to one end of a short stick.

Here are some basic skills with the equipment that anyone can try at home.

## Rope

- Turning the rope forward, jump 25 times.
- Turning the rope backward, jump 25 times.
- Circle the rope over the head, then circle it under the feet with a jump.

## Ball

- Bounce the ball 15 times with the right hand and then 15 times with the left hand.
- Bounce the ball while skipping in a circle.
- Toss the ball into the air, and catch it with two hands behind the back.
- Roll the ball from the right hand to the left hand along both arms and across the chest.

## Hoop

- Circle the hoop around the right hand; circle the

hoop around the left hand.
- Roll the hoop along the ground. Run along beside it and then around it.
- Spin the hoop on the ground and run around it three times before it stops.

## Ribbon

- Write your first name with the ribbon.
- Make little circles with the ribbon.
- Make the ribbon move up and down quickly.
- Make big circles over your head and at your sides.

# The Learning Process

After a gymnast has learned to perform these skills, she may be invited to enroll in a compulsory class.

The compulsory class is the first step toward performing in competition. In compulsories, all of the girls learn the same routines. These routines are choreographed to music, using all the basic skills and dance skills the gymnast learned in classes.

In rhythmic gymnastics, there are three levels of USGF compulsory competition, IV, III and II. Level IV is the easiest and the first stop for a beginning competitor. Level II is the most difficult. Once a gymnast has moved up through the compulsory levels, she can advance to level I, in which she can perform optional routines. That means the gymnast can choreograph her own routine to her own music.

In rhythmic, there are three age divisions for both

< 106 >

*Diane Simpson competed in rhythmic gymnastics at the 1988 Olympics as U.S. national champion.*

compulsory and optional competition. To compete in the children's division a gymnast must be at least 7 years old. A junior gymnast is between 12 and 14, and a senior gymnast is 15 or older. In the U.S., competitions are held for all ages at local, state, and regional levels. Only junior and senior level I gymnasts are able to compete in the national championships.

# Rhythmic Competition

Just as in artistic gymnastics, all rhythmic gymnastics competitions are scored by trained judges, many

< 107 >

of whom were former rhythmic gymnasts themselves. When a judge watches a gymnast perform her routine, she looks for many things: Does the gymnast keep her toes pointed and her knees straight? Can she do her split leaps high into the air? When the gymnast does a turn, does she keep her balance at the end?

In compulsory competition, the judge is also watching if the gymnast does the correct compulsory movements and whether she does them in time to the music.

In the level I optional competition, all gymnasts are required to include certain types of movements in their routines. These are called difficulties. For example, in order to receive a difficulty credit for a toss-and-catch skill with the ball, the gymnast would have to toss the ball high into the air, do two quick turns on her toes, and catch the ball behind her back. With the rope, a difficulty could consist of performing one high split leap in the air while making the rope turn around two times.

In rhythmic, there are two levels of difficulty: medium and superior. (There are no A, B, C, and D ratings as there are in artistic gymnastics.) If a gymnast does a single turn on one foot while making the ribbon do many little circles, she will receive a medium credit. If she does a double turn while performing the same skill, she will receive a superior credit instead.

Optional routines take 60 to 90 seconds. As in artistic gymnastics, the highest score a rhythmic gymnast can receive for a routine is a 10. That means everything the gymnast did was perfect.

A perfect score is difficult to get. Few gymnasts, even Olympians, can say they got a 10! A judge will make deductions for mistakes. These mistakes can be small, medium, or large. A small deduction (.10 or .20 of a point) might be made for a bent knee that was supposed to be straight. A medium deduction (.30 or .40) could be made if a gymnast misses the rope when she was supposed to catch it. A large deduction (.50 and up) could be given if a gymnast drops the ball and must run four or more steps to get it.

# Getting into the Rhythm

Not every girl can become an Olympian like Diane Simpson, but anyone can have fun participating in classes and competitions. If you want to learn more about rhythmic gymnastics, call your local gymnastics club or YWCA and ask if rhythmic classes are available. You may also write to the U.S. Gymnastics Federation at the address at the end of this book.

Because rhythmic gymnastics is still a new sport in the U.S., it is sometimes hard to find rhythmic classes close to your home. But every year, more and more classes are being started throughout the country.

< 109 >

**CHAPTER 8**

# GETTING READY FOR COMPETITION

**W**HETHER YOU GO FOR THE ARTISTIC or the rhythmic variety, the sport of gymnastics will help you develop strength, flexibility, rhythm, graceful movement patterns, and overall body conditioning. But before you begin, it is recommended that you see your family doctor for a physical examination. Your coach should be told of any restrictions that your doctor recommends.

Gymnastics is demanding on the body and can only be enjoyed, and mastered, if your body is well prepared and conditioned. Conditioning simply refers to everything you do to get your body into peak physical condition. A lot of your training and practice in gymnastics will be directed toward increasing flexibility, strength, and endurance. As you improve in these areas, you will find that you learn gymnastics skills quicker, have more energy, and feel more confident in your abilities.

< 110 >

*Someday you may compete in an arena full of fans.*

# Flexibility

When we talk about flexibility, we are talking about the range of motion through which the joints of the body can move without causing pain. Joints are the places where one part of the body is connected to another, like the shoulders and the knees. A gymnast who can hold one of her legs above the forward horizontal position while standing has greater flexibility, strength, and can show a fuller range of motion than another who cannot hold her leg above the horizontal.

Improving your flexibility will help you achieve your gymnastics goals and reduce your chances of getting injured. Gymnasts have different degrees of natural flexibility, but they all can improve with regular training. Some flexibility training programs are:

• **Static stretching.** This is the program we recommend because it is both the safest and easiest method of increasing flexibility. Static stretching uses the force of gravity gradually to increase the stretch of a joint. For example, the gymnast gets into the split position and holds it for anywhere from 30 seconds to five minutes. By the end of that time period, she will notice that her flexibility has increased.

• **PNF (proprioceptive neuromuscular facilitation) stretching.** This also is a good way to increase joint flexibility. However, it must be carefully supervised by a coach. For example, the gymnast again gets into the split position, but in this method, the coach helps her achieve a complete stretch of the joint by pushing on one of her legs. The coach must be careful not to push too hard because a muscle tear or other injury could result.

• **Ballistic stretching.** You will probably hear about this method from other gymnasts or read about it in magazines, but we don't recommend it. That's because it involves active movement, like "bouncing," in the splits. That kind of strain can cause a muscle pull or tear.

Here are some guidelines that will help you in whichever flexibility program you choose:

• Warm up first with easy range-of-motion exercises—arm swings and circles, leg swings, bending—before attempting anything as strenuous as a split.

• Go slowly! Increase your flexibility gradually. It takes time for muscles to increase their capacity to stretch. Forcing them can end in an injury.

• Proper form, position, and mechanics while stretching are essential to prevent an injury.

• Flexibility training should always be combined with an appropriate strength-training program.

# Strength Training

Gymnasts need strength and power to achieve height in their tumbling and vaulting and to move their bodies through complicated—and tiring—routines. Therefore, it is important that each gymnast follow a regular program of strength and power development designed according to her individual needs and supervised by a coach.

There are several ways to increase strength. Calisthenics are exercises that use the gymnast's body weight instead of free weights (dumbbells and barbells) or exercise machines (such as the Nautilus and Universal machines). Many of the exercises used in calisthenics closely resemble gymnastics skills that you will learn. Some examples are push-ups, pull-ups, sit-ups, leg-lifts, and handstand push-ups. In strength training, the exercise is repeated several times to give the muscle group involved a real workout.

Your coach may talk about "sets" and "reps." For example, you might be asked to do 3 sets of 10 repetitions of the basic push-up. This means that you would do 10 push-ups, rest for a bit (10-30 seconds), do another 10 followed by rest, and finish with the third and last set of 10. Altogether, you would have done 30 push-ups. As you develop strength, your coach will gradually increase the number of sets and reps of each exercise to provide a continual challenge to you and your muscles!

Some gymnastics training facilities use free weights or exercise machines in their strength programs. In the past, coaches discouraged weight training because they felt it was not safe for young muscles. Today, however, most strength coaches believe that these methods can provide good results as long as the athletes are carefully instructed and supervised by a qualified person. Here are some basic guidelines:

• Remember to train in a slow, progressive manner, gradually increasing the intensity, length, and rate of exercise.

• Always train and strengthen the large muscle groups, such as the stomach and back muscles, first. They are the foundation for all movement.

• Strength exercises should, as much as possible, closely resemble your gymnastics skills. They should also train each part of the body evenly.

Often, gymnasts find that their muscles are sore the day after strength training. To reduce this problem, gymnasts should stretch immediately after their strength workout. They should also give themselves time to rest after strength training. Rest gives the muscles time to recuperate after a strenuous workout.

< 114 >

# Other Conditioning Programs

Speed and endurance are also very important in gymnastics. Most coaches will say that the fastest runners in the gym are usually the best vaulters. Likewise, speed helps gymnasts reach greater heights in their tumbling runs. In chapter three, we talked about drills that help increase speed. Typical speed drills are sprints over short distances and any other leg exercise that is performed as rapidly as possible.

Endurance is the ability of the body to keep going when it should be getting tired. It comes in handy in long performances and in the final events of a meet. Endurance is developed by performing a movement or an exercise for periods of several minutes. Aerobic dance is an examples of endurance training.

Many gymnasts say conditioning is the hardest part of gymnastics training. But to achieve maximum results, you really must work hard and push yourself. Conditioning is more repetitive and not as much fun as learning new tricks, and progress often seems slow. However, you will find that as you become a better-conditioned gymnast, your confidence will improve and you will find it easier to learn those new skills.

# Gymnastics 'Homework'

Obviously, because of the equipment needed, most of your gymnastics training will take place in the gymnasium. Now and then, however, your coach may assign you some gymnastics homework. There are many strength and flexibility exercises that can be performed at home. For example, you can work on your static stretching or sit-ups while watching TV or even while doing your homework! If you decide to do extra exercises at home, ask your coach which exercises are appropriate and safe to practice without his or her direct supervision.

# The Warm-Up

A good warm-up is essential in getting ready for a gymnastics practice session. A goal of the warm-up is to raise the body temperature. This is most easily accomplished through aerobic-type exercises. Aerobic exercises—like running, skipping, and jumping—make you breathe faster and consume more oxygen.

A well-balanced warm-up combines vigorous movements with light stretching. First, general body movements that involve the large muscle groups are introduced. As the warm-up progresses, basic gymnastics skills—like rolls, handstands, cartwheels, balances, and leaps—may be introduced, too.

The warm-up may take as little as 10 minutes or as long as an hour! At the conclusion of the warm-up you should be completely ready physically (and mentally) for the demands of your first event workout. A good sign that the warm-up has been effective is that you are breathing hard.

< 116 >

# Workouts

What is a typical gymnastics workout like? Let's have a look.

A gymnast always begins her workout with a warm-up that generally lasts anywhere from 10 to 30 minutes. After that, she moves from one event to another, spending anywhere from 30 to 60 minutes at each.

During the individual-event training, the gymnast works on skill elements and practices routines. Often, the coach will end each workout with a short, special-ized strength-training exercise. For example, at the end of the bar workout, the athletes might do chin-ups and leg-lifts.

After the event workout, it is time to work on either strength or flexibility training. These are often alter-nated from day-to-day to allow the gymnast a recov-ery, or rest, period. For example, the gymnast might do her strength training on Monday, Wednesday, and Friday and her flexibility training on Tuesday and Thursday.

The length of a training session can be anywhere from one-and-a-half to six hours per day. It depends on the availability of facilities and the skill level and age of the gymnast. If you "make the team," you can expect to spend 9 to 15 hours per week training for competition. World-class gymnasts typically train 25 to 30 (or more!) hours per week.

< 117 >

# What Happens In a Meet?

Okay, you've been learning and training, and now you're ready. Let's imagine that you are about to compete in your first USGF level 5 gymnastics meet.

The day before the meet, your coach will call the team members together to review just what they should expect during the competition and to make suggestions about how to get ready for it. He or she will tell you that you should eat normally on the day before the meet, but high on the carbohydrate side and low on the fats. Also, you should get to bed early so that you will be rested and ready!

On the morning of the meet, you should eat a good, nutritious breakfast, on the light side—moderate portions with low fats, such as cold cereal, whole wheat toast or a bagel, fruit or juice. You are probably going to be nervous, so you don't want to eat anything that might give you problems with your digestion. Before you leave home, double check that you have everything you need: floor music cassette, two leotards, team warm-up suit, handgrips, athletic tape.

When you arrive at the competition site, you and your teammates will each receive a number that you pin onto the back of your leotard. After a short, general warm-up time, your squad will go through a timed warm-up period at each of the four events to practice your routines. Each gymnast usually gets about two minutes on each apparatus. When that's over, all of the teams will line up and march in to be presented

< 118 >

formally to the audience and the judges. After the national anthem, each squad will march to its first assigned event.

Teams are assigned to their first, or start, event by a random draw and then proceed through the four events in Olympic order: vault, bars, beam, floor. Gymnasts at every level always compete in sequence.

While waiting for your turn, continue to stretch and keep warm by rehearsing basic movements on the sidelines or in the area provided by the meet directors. Be ready for your turn! The head judge will indicate when you are to begin your routine by raising a green flag.

Now you are up! At the green-flag signal, the gymnast raises one or both arms over her head and then turns to take her place to begin her routine. Do your best! At the end of your routine, be sure to salute the head judge. This is not the same kind of salute that a soldier gives to his commander; the gymnast merely stands with good posture facing the head judge.

You're not done yet. Now you have to prepare for your next event!

At the conclusion of the meet is the awards ceremony. It is traditional that all of the gymnasts accept their awards in leotards or warm-up suits. Please, no street clothes or T-shirts! Depending upon the level and size of the meet, awards might include ribbons and/or medals based upon the order in which the gymnasts finished in their events. For example, the first place finisher would receive a gold medal, second a sil-

< 119 >

ver, third a bronze medal, fourth a red ribbon.

In the USGF level 5 competitions, the awards given are all based upon the gymnast's score in an event. Anyone scoring below a 7.0 gets a participation ribbon, 7.0-7.45 a yellow ribbon, 7.5-7.95 a white ribbon, 8.0-8.95 a red ribbon, and 9.0 and over a blue. In the all-around competition, any score below 29.00 receives a participation ribbon, 29.00-30.95 a yellow, 31.00-32.95 a white, 33.00-34.95 a red, and 35.00 and over a blue.

Collect your medals and ribbons and take a bow. Congratulations! Now you are truly part of the team.

For additional information, you can write to
The United States Gymnastics Federation
Pan American Plaza, Suite 300
201 S. Capitol Avenue
Indianapolis, IN 46225
or call
Tel: 317-237-5050.

*Making the team doesn't just bring medals and flowers; it can make you fit and confident, too.*

< 121 >

# GLOSSARY

**Acrobatic movements:** umbrella term to describe tumbling skills, including cartwheels, handsprings, and saltos

**Aerial:** a type of move in which the gymnast turns completely over in the air without touching the apparatus with her hands, as in an aerial cartwheel

**Afterflight:** in vaulting, the flight from the horse to the landing

**Amplitude:** the height, or degree of stretch or extension, of the body when performing a move

**Apparatus:** one of the various pieces of equipment in gymnastic events

**Arabesque:** a body position in which the gymnast stands on one foot, with the free leg held in the rear at an angle of 45 degrees, or more, to the support leg

**Arabian salto:** a somersault with a half twist that requires the gymnast, who begins facing forward, to finish facing backward, or vice versa

**Arch:** a position with the body curved backward

**Ball:** as a handheld apparatus in rhythmic gymnastics, the ball measures about seven inches (18-20 centimeters) in diameter and is thrown, caught, bounced, and rolled during a routine

**Cartwheel:** a trick performed on the floor or balance

beam in which the gymnast imitates the turn of a wheel; she does a quarter-turn to face sideways, passes through a handstand by placing the hands alternately on the floor, and steps out onto her feet

**Cast:** on the uneven bars, a straight body swing to start movement

**Choreography:** the arrangement of movements to music, as in dance or a rhythmic gymnastics routine

**Clear:** on the uneven bars, a movement in which only the hands (not the body) touch the apparatus

**Club:** as a handheld apparatus in rhythmic gymnastics, the club measures between 15½ and 19½ inches (40-50 centimeters) long, weighs 5¼ ounces (150 grams); and is tossed, tapped, circled from the shoulders, elbows and wrists, and windmilled—usually two at a time

**Composition:** the arrangement of required skills in a gymnastics routine

**Compulsories:** routines that contain specific movements required of all gymnasts

**Demi-plié:** a position of the legs and feet used in preparation for jumps and turns and in landings, with knees bent and the knees and feet turned outward

**Difficulty:** in judging, the measure of how challenging a skill is, with skills divided into four levels of difficulty—$A$, $B$, $C$, and $D$; level $A$ is the easiest and $D$ the most difficult

**Dismount:** the act of leaving an apparatus at the end of a routine, usually with a twist or a somersault

**Endurance:** the ability to keep up a high level of energy for a long period of time

**Execution:** the performance of a routine

**Flexibility:** the range of movement of a part of the body, such as an arm or a leg, without feeling pain

**Flip:** turning over one full rotation in the air, feet over head, without the support of the arms; it can be done forward, backward, or sideways

**Giant swing:** on the uneven bars, a motion during which the body is fully extended and moving through a 360-degree rotation around the higher bar

**Gymnastics movements:** those skills from dance and rhythmic gymnastics—including leaps, turns, and jumps—that have been categorized by difficulty

**Handspring:** pushing off the hands into a flip, either forward or backward

**Hitch kick:** jumping from one foot to the other while switching legs with a scissorslike motion in front of the body

**Hurdle:** a long and powerful skip that launches the gymnast onto the vault springboard or into a balance-beam or floor-exercise move

**Inverted:** a position in which the head is down and the legs are up

**Kip:** on the uneven bars, a basic movement that uses the pike position to propel the gymnast from a hang position (below the bar) into a support position (above it)

**Layout:** a position in which the body is held straight or slightly arched

**Locomotor movements:** basic motions that allow the body to cover ground, such as walking, running, skipping, and hopping

**Lunge:** a position in which one leg is bent at the knee in a demi-plié position and the other leg is extended backward, with the body held erect over the flexed leg

**Optionals:** routines that are designed by and for the individual gymnast to show off her skills

**Over-grip:** on the uneven bars, holding on with hands on top of bar, palms forward

**Passé:** a standing position in which the toes of one foot touch the ankle of the other foot; a French word meaning "to cross"

**Pike:** a position in which the body is bent forward at the waist more than 90 degrees while the legs are kept straight

**Pirouette:** a turn of 360 degrees, or more, on one leg; also the same turn on the hands in the handstand position, or while in the air on a jump

**Preflight:** in vaulting, the jump motion from the board to the horse

**Release:** on the uneven bars, letting go of a bar to perform a move

**Relevé:** a standing position in which the gymnast rises up on the balls of her feet; a French word meaning "to rise"

**Ribbon:** as a handheld apparatus in rhythmic gymnastics, the ribbon is about 19½ feet (6 meters) long and is tossed and caught and used to make snaking, spiraling, circling, and figure-eight patterns

**Rope:** in rhythmic gymnastics, the rope is cut to a length in proportion to the height of the gymnast and is tossed, caught, and leapt through

**Roundoff:** a cartwheel in which the gymnast makes an additional quarter-turn and lands on both feet to end up facing the direction she came from; it is a move used to change direction in a balance beam or floor exercise routine

**Routine:** a combination of tricks on one apparatus that allows the gymnast to display a range of skills

**Salto:** a forward or back flip or somersault, with the feet coming up over the head

**Split:** a position in which legs are extended front to back at an angle of 180 degrees

**Spot:** assistance for a gymnast while performing a movement, particularly when she is learning, by guiding her through it or preventing her from falling; usually done by a coach

**Stag jump:** a split leap during which the forward leg is bent at the knee and the trailing leg is extended backward

**Stalder circle:** on the uneven bars, a forward or backward circle from handstand to handstand, in a straddle position; it is named for the gymnast who first performed it

**Stick:** to land without moving the feet

**Straddle:** a position in which the legs are extended sideways

**Tsukahara:** a family of vaults in which the gymnast executes a half-turn onto the horse and then a backward salto, with or without a twist, in the afterflight; it is named for the gymnast who first performed it

**Tuck:** a basic position in which the upper body is flexed at the hips and the knees are bent

**Tumbling:** an umbrella term that describes the acrobatic elements—saltos, roundoffs, cartwheels—performed in series on the balance beam and in the floor exercise; it is also a competitive artistic gymnastics event, but not one of the four Olympic events

**Turn-out:** a position in which the legs are rotated outward at the hips

**Twist:** a complete spin of the body from side to side

**Under-grip:** on the uneven bars, holding on with the hands on top of the bar, palms toward the gymnast; this is also called a reverse grip

**Walkout:** a landing in which the gymnast lands with alternate foot placement, as if walking; it can be forward or backward

**Yamishita:** a family of vaults similar to the handspring, except the body is in pike position, then stretched in the afterflight